TIME BANDIT

Two Brothers, the Bering Sea,

Andy and Johnathan Hillstrand

with Malcolm MacPherson

BANDIT

and One of the World's Deadliest Jobs

BALLANTINE BOOKS | NEW YORK

2009 Ballantine Books Trade Paperback Edition

Published in the United States by Ballantine Books,
an imprint of The Random House Publishing Group,
a division of Random House, Inc., New York.

BALLANTINE and colophon are registered trademarks of
Random House, Inc.

Originally published in hardcover in the United States by
Ballantine Books, an imprint of The Random House Publishing Group,
a division of Random House, Inc., in 2008.

Library of Congress Cataloging-in-Publication Data

Hillstrand, Andy.
Time bandit : two brothers, the Bering Sea, and one of the world's
deadliest jobs / Andy and Johnathan Hillstrand, with Malcolm
MacPherson.
p. cm.
ISBN 978-0-345-50412-8
1. Alaskan king crab fisheries—Bering Sea.   2. Hillstrand, Andy.
3. Hillstrand, Johnathan.   I. Hillstrand, Johnathan.   II. MacPherson,
Malcolm.   III. Title.

SH380.45.B47H55 2008
639'.570922—dc22
2007052363

Printed in the United States of America

www.ballantinebooks.com

Book design by Liz Cosgrove

For Dad. We miss you.

To my wife, Sabrina, thanks for sticking with me through thick and thin for twenty-six years. I love you. To my daughters, Chelsey and Cassie, you make me proud to be your dad. To the rest of my family, thanks for the great memories.

—Andy

To our grandmother, Jo, and our mother, Joan, (along with our step-father, Bob, and all the other people I am so blessed to have in my life), for your love and for helping me to raise my son, Scotty, all the times I was gone.

—Johnathan

Contents

TIME BANDIT

I Live Like a King

Johnathan

I am a fisherman, an Alaskan fisherman, and a Bering Sea crab fisherman with thirty-seven years on commercial boats. I am tagged as a "bad boy of the Bering Sea" in "the deadliest profession in America." I have fought forty-foot seas and seen rogue waves one hundred feet high. I work on water cold enough to kill a man in five minutes, and I have bent under the power of 120-knot Williwaw winds and watched the crushing strength of the Arctic ice pack move south from Russia around the hull of my boat, *Time Bandit*. I am Johnathan Hillstrand and that is where I stand in the universe.

Right now, that might be another man's life, because I am drifting in a small boat without power, alone, and with no help in sight. Waves no taller than my forearm lap the hull with a rhythm that makes me want to dream. Nothing here threatens me. The sky is a washed-out blue without a cloud to the horizon in every direction.

It's creeping me out.

The boat I am on, a thirty-eight-foot Weggley gill-netter I named fishing vessel (F/V) *Fishing Fever*, bobs with the tide in full ebb at about four knots. The boat and I are captives of a moon that pulls us southwestward. I am, I can only estimate, fifty to sixty miles southwest of the mouth of the Kasilof River where I started this morning. I have about ten dozen fat, fresh, Cook Inlet, red sockeye salmon on ice in my tanks. I care where the tide is drifting me (not just because going where I do not want to go is an inconvenience); I would prefer to be back at fishing camp by nightfall with my buddies in the junkyard behind the Kasilof cannery with a bottle of Crown Royal in one hand and a hot dog in the other, telling stories around an oil-drum fire. Almost certainly, that will not happen.

I started drifting when *Fishing Fever*'s engine blew up more than three hours ago. The reduction gear fried with a grunt, and the boat shuddered and died like it had been sapped. The demise did not come as a complete surprise. The boat's former owner never changed the oil, and the engine was flooded twice. I bought the boat four years ago because I liked the shape of its hull, not the thrum of its engine. The blame is also mine. I had gunned the engine at stressful rpms back and forth along the hundred-yard length of the gill net in an attempt to herd the spawning salmon toward the mesh. I cannot make repairs to the reduction gear until I can get back to Kasilof, lay the boat on the mud, and get a mechanic in the tiny engine compartment with wrenches. I opened up the cover and squeezed myself—I am 6′ 1″ and weigh 205 pounds—behind the drive shaft for a look. The shaft is not spinning, and clear oil leaks in the reduction gear when I turn the engine off. Murphy's Law works on water as well as on land. My batteries are not charging. I am leaking power slowly. With batteries fading, no motor, no radios, I am, in a word, fucked.

I shut the cover, wishing I could forget what I saw.

The tide is drifting me faster than I like in the direction of Augustine Island and beyond, into the Shelikof Strait, where anything can happen, and sometimes does. In his ship's log, Captain Cook supposedly wrote that the second worst weather and currents on earth, after Cape Horn, can be found in the Strait. Like the Bering Sea where my brother and I fish, storms come up in the Strait with startling speed and a violence that can turn a pond into a maelstrom in six hours, and often less. The winds whip off the icy fjord walls that overlook the Strait; currents from the Kennedy Entrance compete with currents from the Cook Inlet, Kachemak Bay, the Gulf of Alaska, and several tidal rips. Put together, these produce swells like nowhere else in Alaska. I look at my watch. As we say, shit happens when you party naked.

It was not long ago that I was caught in the Strait. It was blowing eighty. I looked out and shouted into an indifferent and wild wind. I was coming in to shelter in a cove when I saw a man on the water in what looked like a canoe. He was waving a red coat. I did not believe my eyes. My deckhand and friend, Codfish Tom, woke up and looked to verify the sight. Codfish is a big dude with a head big enough to have its own gravity, its own atmosphere, its own weather system. I asked him, "Do you see that, Codfish?"

He said, "It doesn't make sense."

Three guys were sitting on the *bottom* of a boat no bigger than *Fishing Fever;* the storm had capsized their craft with only the bow sticking out. The men were dying slowly of hypothermia, bleeding out body warmth twenty-four times faster than they would in air the same temperature as the water. A bitter cold was reaching its icy fingers into the core of their hearts. They had no survival suits. I jumped into the water in my survival suit to save them. They had no strength when I reached them. One of them sank. He just gave up and headed to the bottom. I grabbed him by the hair and pulled him up for breath. One by one I brought them onboard my boat and gave them hot coffee and cigarettes and dry clothes. I quickly flipped through the pages in a book for advice on treating hypothermia, where I learned that under no circumstances was I to give them coffee or cigarettes. I smacked the smokes out of their mouths. One guy could not talk he was so cold. I kept asking him, "What's your name? Tell me your name," to keep him alive. The man I pulled out by the hair later tattooed the name of my boat on his arm: *Arctic Nomad*.

We sheltered in that cove, with them aboard, until the storm subsided. There was nothing else we could do.

So I know the weather in the Strait. I know about the cold and what Alaskan waters can do. The Coast Guard does not mandate 406/121.5 MHZ EPIRBs, an Emergency Position Indicating Radio Beacon, on boats the size of *Fishing Fever*. EPIRBs automatically beam a Mayday and identifying signal and location to a satellite and down to the Coast Guard in Juneau. Without an EPIRB, I might as well not exist in a crisis. Not that the Coast Guard would tow me in if they knew, unless I was about to go under; maritime law assigns liability for a broken boat to the boat that tows her in, and the Coast Guard, while a reassuring presence, does not view itself as AAA.

Making matters worse, *Fishing Fever* does not carry a single sideband radio; no other boat in the Cook Inlet red salmon fleet does either. My VHF went screwy when the engine quit; I have been losing batteries all morning (and besides, VHF channel 16 reaches only about 20 miles). My Razr cell phone could not find a signal this far out in the bland wilderness of the sea even if I had not thrown it on the oil-drum fire last night. By the time I fished it out of the flames it looked like a s'more. At least as far as technology goes, I would be better off right now in the era of James Cook with sail, sextant, and pennant signal flags.

I stayed up last night getting drunk. I stopped counting at eighteen double shots. There is too much Crown Royal in this world and not enough willpower. I was out of control. At the camp, my fellow drift netters and I decided to fish the next day according to where we threw magnetic darts at a silhouette of a naked woman we had drawn on the side of a broken-down white van. I hit the lower regions, which put me down on the south line for the opening. With that much decided, we talked about what we talk about at fishing camp—fishing, boats, gadgets, and women, in that order. We did not get to the topic of women before the Crown Royal got to me. The last thing I remember, I was telling my buddies about the time my brother Andy and I were fishing for red king crabs in Bristol Bay. We were trying an experiment with a TV camera that we had contained in a watertight box that we were towing underwater to help us locate crabs, which roll along the sea floor in balls fifteen feet high. Sometimes they migrate as many as four miles in a day. Andy and I were staring into the TV monitor when suddenly a human arm floated by wearing the orange sleeve of a seaman's rain slicker, with a blue rubber glove on its hand. Where the rest of the body went, who could say?

"Did you see *that*?" I asked Andy.

He said, "I saw it. Did *you* see it?"

We started to laugh—a psychotic, not a funny, laugh. Just then, at that exact moment, we felt a bump against the hull. We told each other it might be the rest of the guy looking for his arm. But we had only bumped into a humpback whale, and he was mad as hell. On the surface, he glared at us with a huge eyeball that seemed to be telling us, "Next time watch where you're going, Bub."

Last night, I staggered from the fishing camp to the river, took a skiff out to *Fishing Fever*, tied to a buoy in the channel—around midnight, as I recall—and slept on the bunk in the back of the wheelhouse until three this morning when I cast off the buoy. Fishing was set to open at seven and would close twelve hours later. I did not want to be a minute late. My friends from camp followed me out through the darkness into the Inlet. At this moment, while I drift, they are netting their catch somewhere out of sight to the northeast of me.

To me, gillnetting salmon *is* fishing. I hate to miss a minute of the fun. I fish for red king and opilio crabs in winter to help pay for salmon netting in summer. I never can seem to make money off salmon. I do not know why. And I really do not care. I love the camp, the guys, the fish, and the fishing. To me the pleasures are worth breaking even. Sockeye salmon are the most beautiful fish in the world. They are the first to come upriver and are the biggest and nicest. This year I will get $1.10 a pound for them. But that is not what draws me out on the water year after year. The ritual of catching them reminds me of the old ways: One man, one boat, and one sea. Unlike crab fishing on the Bering Sea, with salmon netting there are no hydraulic booms, pot launchers, 800-pound pots, or coilers, no deck crew and pot blocks. The process, blissful for its simplicity, has not changed for a century.

Once out where the salmon are rushing in from the sea, I watch the surface of the water for jumpers. Salmon grow excited near the mouth of the river where they were born. After years at sea they know they are fast approaching the end of their life's amazing journey. They come toward the land in schools of hundreds and thousands, dodging men like me who are out to stop them. The ones nearest the surface jump and slap the water with their tails, I like to think, in celebration of the closing circle of their lives. They are going to die soon but in dying in the fresh waters where they were born they are renewing life, and I like to think that this renewal gives them profound joy.

I watch their direction, race my boat ahead, roll the net off the reel, and wait for them to hit. The net by law can be no more than thirty-two feet deep. If a salmon is large, it cannot enter the webbing, and if small, it swims cleanly through. The right size fish is trapped and cannot back out without snagging its gills. The trick for me is to get them onto the boat quickly, before the screaming gulls pluck out their eyes and the seals bite chunks out of their blood-red flesh. And if they are not bled soon, their blood spoils and alters the flavor of their flesh.

As fast as I can, I turn the reel, pick the fish out of the net, and turn some more until the net is wound around, and the fish are flapping at my ankles. In the sun their skin shines silver with shadows of black and shades of gray. They are two to three feet long, sleek and firm, brimming with healthy wild life. They are what God meant fish to be, the king of fish and not just because English kings used to be the only ones allowed to fish them. They bestow a grace on me. I live like a king, I believe, thanks to the blessings of wild salmon.

It looks like I may be filleting one from the hold for lunch. But for now, I enter the cabin from the deck and stretch out on the bunk in the wheelhouse, cushioned by a sleeping bag, with a pillow under my head, with nothing to do but wait and think and reminisce. The time will not be wasted.

In another two months, my brother Andy and I will start our twenty-eighth continuous season crabbing on the Bering Sea. Since I ended the 2006–2007 crab season last March, I have not taken stock of all that happened to me. In its broadest outlines, last year was by far the wildest, most bizarre, stressful, and joyous of my life. Fateful forces aligned to both greet and bushwhack me. There were storms in my stars. I put a man in a coma for three days with my fists and feet—and nearly killed him— over the honor of a woman. I spent Christmas and New Year's in jail facing a maximum sentence of ten years. Somewhere along the line a complete stranger told me she had never seen so many angels as she saw over my head—and she swore she could see them her whole life. On the Bering Sea, my brother Andy and I plugged *Time Bandit*'s tanks with red king crab and opilio. I saved a man's life by plucking him from the icy clutches of the Bering Sea. The Arctic ice pack off the Pribilof Islands nearly crushed the steel hull of *Time Bandit*, with me in command.

Over the course of last year, my brother and I spit in the devil's eye. If the devil lives anywhere, he lives on the Bering Sea. And though we did not sail to the end of the earth, we glimpsed its ledge over our bow. I yelled and screamed and laughed and cried tears of sorrow and relief. My legs quaked with fear. I drank an ocean of whiskey, smoked Winstons until I choked, became a grandfather twice over, made love to women whom I won't soon forget, and by the season's end was set adrift, now, helpless as a beached whale.

Andy and I started our usual crab fishing season in September last year in the same place where we started our lives. A sleepy fishing village that wanders along a low bluff facing the Kachemak Bay in the Lower Cook Inlet, Homer is rooted in the same character that the Sourdoughs brought with them when they settled Alaska back in the day. Barely a week goes by when I do not remind myself of just how different Andy and I might have turned out if we had been born elsewhere. I would probably be in jail; Andy would be a cowboy. We *are* different from the rest of mankind, for better and for worse, because of the influences that started out with Homer Pennock, a charming—and none too clever—nineteenth-century confidence trickster whose cussedness and eccentricity put a stamp on his namesake town forever after. Barely a soul in Homer—there are 5,000 of us now—has not invented the narrative of his life, just like Pennock. The trick of adapting on the fly makes the hard Alaskan climate and harsh terrain easier for people, who come up to Homer— and Alaska in general—to meet their full expectations of independence and hardiness. A place like Homer offers them just the right measure of freedom to breathe as they see fit.

One feature dominates Homer with the same force with which Pennock pressed himself on the town. My brothers and I grew up living on a narrow finger of sand and rock laid down by a retreating glacier eons ago. Called the Spit, this odd geological feature juts five miles into Kachemak Bay, and put us boys *out to sea*, on land, as soon as we could crawl. We grew up with salt air in our lungs and sand between our toes. We played with eels and crabs and dog sharks. Instead of bicycles, we moved by skiff and raft. We did not play at being cowboys. We were pirates of yore. We knew an endless sea as other kids knew their backyards. The sea formed the stuff of our make-believe lives. We dreamed of ships and sails, demons and dragons.

Our father fed us and bought our clothes out of the ocean's bounty. His friends went to the sea. My grandfather Earl, who was a lawyer and politician and a weekend fisherman, had built the Land's End Inn on the Spit and owned the legendary Salty Dawg saloon, a cavelike log-cabin haunt where, as kids, we played in the sawdust on the floor and overheard drunken sailors' yarns. Huckleberry Finn had the Mississippi River, islands in the streams, and woods on the shores. But we had the sea, which gave us his same utter freedom to explore, dream, and be boys without adults to shrink us down to their size. Huck had his thing, but he never had sharks to poke with a stick and shrimp and salmon to catch and cook over a rock fire in tinfoil and skiffs to push into the water from the front door of Miss Watson's house.

Sometimes we would trap Dungeness crabs and trade them with Max Deveney, who owned a small seafood shop in Homer. He gave us one cooked crab for two fresh ones, and we went back and forth from the Spit into town several times a day, checking our pots and trading with Deveney, who sometimes even paid us a dollar a fish for salmon. Once we saved $109. We thought we were millionaires. We bought a case of Ding Dongs, a case of Mars bars, and a case of Hershey bars. Candy by the case! That was the stuff our dreams were made of.

Once, at night, camping on the other side of the Inlet, we pitched our tents at the base of an embankment. We lit a fire and roasted a crow and a squirrel. We were sitting on some of the best-tasting mussels on earth but we did not know that they could be eaten. Nobody had told us. We went to bed. It was dark, of course, and we were more scared of the dark than we would admit. At some point, I woke up when something hit my tent. Then something else hit my tent. I did not know what it was, and I was afraid to find out. In another minute, I felt something furry crawling on my face. We began screaming like girls in a scary movie. These creepy things were all over the tent, inside and out. I turned on a flashlight. It was raining *lemmings*.

Over the years people who lived in Homer acquired another quality that was a by-product of the sea. It was a sense of impending loss. The feeling was ancient, as old as when men first ventured off land. Nobody ever got used to the premature death of men at sea but after a long time and many losses, a certain resignation had seeped into the collective Homer mind. The men tried to deny it. They thought of drowning as tragic but honorable, as a tribute that had to be paid to nature and the devils of the Bering Sea. The fear of loss never left some part of the thoughts of every man and woman in Homer, whether or not they earned their livings off the sea. It created a pervasive mood of melancholy. But loss at sea also made men of the sea wild, with an abandonment of normal habits and thoughts. We were here today and gone tomorrow because we knew that was what we were, and we lived the here today to its fullest. Yet death followed us, like a spy.

About the time I came into the world, in 1962, Homer was going through rough times. A dirt road that connected the town to the outside world was not paved until the 1970s, and people came and went more conveniently by sea. In those days, Homer meant a hardscrabble existence. But soon its natural beauty and isolation attracted eccentrics fleeing conformity, the law, and convention. Hippies discovered the town early in the Sixties and spread their anarchist gospel. Artists and a sprinkling of poets and writers followed. A colony of "Barefooters" pitched up with the vow not to wear shoes, to let their hair grow, and dress in cotton robes until peace was achieved in the world. "Old Believers," nonconformist sectarians of the Russian Orthodox Church, came next with their own peculiar devotion. The most celebrated local eccentric now is a sweet older woman named Jean Keene, also known as "The Eagle Lady." She lives on the Spit in the tiniest of log cabins where she cares for the feeding of bald eagles, which flock around her house from as far away as Kodiak. She is a savvy, rugged septuagenarian, Alaskan to the core, who drives a rusted, beaten Chevy pickup and works in a cannery. She would not live anywhere else.

Getting away from government drew others to Homer like Cook Inlet sockeye draw me to the sea each summer. That was surely the case with my old man and his friends. LeRoy Shoultz, for instance, a neighbor and friend, decided to leave the Lower Forty-Eight when the Indiana police called to warn him of a summons. A neighbor had turned him in for leaving his trashcan out by the curb. That same night he told his young wife, Rita, "OK, that's enough of this stuff," and packed up his young family without further deliberation. With $1,100 in his wallet and a credit card for gas he hit the highway, not that he was leaving that much behind. To his way of thought, Indiana was old and settled. Alaska was wild, and he yearned for its promise. When he and his family reached Alaska, even the air tasted free. He was flat broke, with four young kids, a couple cans of beans, and some oatmeal to live on, but they all considered nothing too hard in exchange for adventure and freedom from in-your-face government.

New friends in campgrounds gave them salmon to get by on. "We weren't complaining," I remember Rita telling me. She assumed that work would turn up for LeRoy. A local carpenter saw their Indiana license plate and invited them home to a moose dinner. He recommended LeRoy to the local cannery. With LeRoy now employed, they rented a one-room shack in town for $50 a month, with one bed. Rita told me, "We thought we were living high. We had electricity and a rain barrel for water. In a little while we had enough to build a small log cabin. After we first moved in, my mom came up to visit us from Indiana, and I was just totally excited that we had a driveway. We had no water, just electricity. But *we had a driveway*. My mom could not get that into her head. She just couldn't understand that up here you are fighting everyday things all the time. You have to be young *all the time*."

As Rita said, nowhere more than in Alaska, the land formed people with sharp, chiseled features. The extremes of weather—minus-80 degree temperatures, Williwaw winds that blew 130 mph, and 90 inches of snowfall a year—made Alaskans seem almost foreign to their more genteel cousins in the Lower Forty-Eight. Alaska presented a blank slate to write lives anew. All that was needed was grit. The cold and dark of Alaskan winters made us naturally cussed, independent, and self-reliant, which in turn gave us a lottery mentality—if somebody was going to win, why shouldn't it be me?

And, in keeping, we strictly did not ask for outside help. In Alaska, people reached out to their neighbors. Charity and neighborliness were not virtues that we practiced only on Sundays. And nothing brought that home to us in Homer more than the loss of the trawler *Aleutian Harvester.*

At the time, Thanksgiving 1985, I was fishing with my dad by the Augustine volcano, and we had sheltered up in a storm. With not much else to do but ride it out, I talked on single sideband radio to a friend aboard the *Aleutian Harvester* named Danny Martin. I had worked for two or three seasons with Danny on a gill net boat named *Sea Hawk II.* That day he was fishing near us, and I asked him how it was going. He said, "It sucks, man. This is my last trip." He was net dragging in forty- or fifty-foot waves, and he should not have been out there. A while later I heard a Mayday on the radio. *Aleutian Harvester* had been on radar, and then, in the blink of an eye, she was gone. She had rolled over and vanished like a stone down a well. No one at first could understand. She went too quickly. Nobody in Homer, where three of the four *Harvester* crewmen came from, wanted to believe that a ship of that size could vanish in plain sight with its sister ship only an eighth of a mile off. There were no survivors, no flotsam, no jetsam, not a single trace that the *Aleutian* had ever existed. The Coast Guard searched for three days with helicopters, airplanes, and boats before they quit. But the people of Homer were not yet ready to abandon their own sons. If you are a relative or friend of a man lost at sea, there can be no time limit on loss. Homerites stuffed money in hats, emptied savings accounts, liquidated stocks, and held fund-raisers to pay for private search helicopters and airplanes that cost $5,000 a day. That effort to find any trace of the *Harvester*—and nothing was ever found—

started the Aleutian Harvester Fund, which since 1985 has paid for pilots to search for lost airplanes, stranded tourists, and hunters, and sadly, other sailors on ships lost at sea.

A family friend tells a story that my brothers and I repeat often. Ken Moore, who owns the Northern Enterprises Boatyard in Homer where I dry-dock *Fishing Fever* over the winter, owed a debt of gratitude to a couple named Mudd and Stinky Jones who had come to Homer, as Ken says, "without a sink." Stinky was a carpenter whose idea of finished work was with a chain saw. Later, after Mudd left him, he lived in two partially buried steel tanks. At the time, the couple owned a devil's half acre out of town but more often than not stayed in Homer in a house borrowed from a friend named Poop Deck Platt. Ken was working two jobs at that time, driving back and forth between Homer and Kenai, up the peninsula. One day, Stinky asked Ken to pick up something in Anchor Point on his weekly commute. Several days went by, and while driving through Clam Gulch, Ken remembered the favor. He had forgotten the specifics. He stopped at the Anchor River Inn to call Stinky on the phone. There, he faced an embarrassing dilemma. Who *was* Stinky Jones? In a phone book he found six Joneses with telephones in the Homer area, but Ken had no idea who Stinky was. He called each Jones, asking, "Are you Stinky?" After three numbers he heard a familiar voice. His first question, "What's your *name*, Stinky?" It was Karl.

Ken, who is my father's age, knew men who went by Popeye, a sailor; Pappy, Popeye's pappy; Packsack Louie; Ike the Kike; and Hundred Log Tallis. That was how mail was addressed to them. Hardly anybody knew Poop Deck as Clarence. He used to say, "Nobody remembers Clarence, and nobody forgets Poop Deck."

But Homer was not all sweetness. Everyone knew everyone else, and that was good in a crisis. But there was no anonymity like city dwellers enjoy. Gossip crushed even people who were strong. And privacy was difficult to come by. A few years ago, a local Homer character, a drunk and a vagrant, acquired an annoying habit. He would drop by houses unannounced at unexpected times and act as if he owned the place. He would pour a cocktail, stay awhile, and leave when he was ready. That went on for years. Most people locked their doors. But some never bothered to. They complained to a judge who ordered the man to behave. On the next Thanksgiving, a family in town was sitting down to a festive meal when the drunk arrived and refused to leave. The father politely rose from the table and went for a gun. He shot the man dead in the living room. Pondering what sentence to give the killer, who pled guilty, a local judge sentenced him to one month in the town jail. In Homer, hospitality and neighborliness should be expected but not taken for granted.

Only the wild animals were run out of town. Around Homer, bears killed people and moose chased people, and that brings to mind my Grandmother Jo, who feared neither man nor beast. She and her husband, our maternal grandfather, Ernie Shupert, were Alaska homesteaders, original settlers after the Second World War to whom the United States government gave land. In return, they planted alfalfa and later, rhubarb and strawberries and built a small log house on eighty acres. Grandfather Ernie had served with Col. Lawrence Castner's "Cutthroats," officially the Alaska Combat Intelligence Platoon: sixty-four scouts, snipers, and irregulars who fought the Japanese forces garrisoned on two islands at the western end of the Aleutian chain. He decided, after the war, to stay in Alaska.

Grandma Jo came from Southern California. She is a delicate woman with the heart of a dragon who tarred the roof of her house when she was in her eighties. After Ernie died, the government forbade her to bury him at home. She stormed down to the county offices and told the supervisor, "I'm doing it. If you want to dig him up, then dig him up, but he's *going in*." Grandpa Shupert still lies there by the driveway.

We often stayed with Grandma Jo and Grandpa Ernie in the summers in our preteen years when our father was out fishing. Grandpa Ernie shot two bears from the door of the house one summer. He dressed them and hung their carcasses from a tripod; they looked just like skinned humans and the sight haunted me. From then on, I had bear nightmares. We ate bear meat, and Grandpa Ernie cured the hides for blankets. Their bathroom was an outhouse about fifty yards across dangerous bear terrain. When nature called in the middle of the night, I could beat the speed of light getting to that outhouse. More than once, a bear loomed out of the moonlight, and I sat shouting for help until the bear moved on.

Even though she is now ninety-one and weighs no more than eighty pounds, Grandma Jo faced down a moose alone not long ago when she was walking down her sloped driveway with her little dog Allie, who loved to eat pancakes. Grandma Jo was picking up the mail on the Sterling Highway, where she lives about five miles north of Homer on forested land, when a moose cow stepped out of the trees onto the gravel drive. At first she was worried that the animal was a bear; she was less afraid of a moose. She hurried her pace, looking back over her shoulder, and did not see a bull moose standing almost in front of her until it was too late.

He charged her, knocking her flat on the snow. Grandma was unconscious. She woke up in an instant to see the moose rising on its rear legs to attack her with its front hooves, and she thought, "This is it." But her dog Allie barked and snarled and frightened the animal away. He stood guard over Grandma Jo and then helped her back to the house. Grandma did not think she was injured in the attack. She drank a cup of tea in her kitchen and turned on the TV. She enjoys game shows. When our brother Neal insisted that she visit the hospital, just in case, she found excuses until he drove her into Homer days later. The doctors said she had cracked her ribs. She still refused to believe that she was hurt. Neal asked her if she would rather live closer to town for safety's sake. "I wouldn't live anywhere else," she told him, which ended that discussion.

Living off nature, indeed being *in* nature, drew people closer to life and death in Alaska than in other places. Whether it was a Sunday picnic or sport fishing for halibut, the most intense fun came from the excitement of near disaster. Not long ago, friends and I traveled Homer's shoreline on four-wheelers on a picnic around a point that floods at high tide. A tree branch swept one friend off his four-wheeler and knocked him senseless. A woman lost her camera. A kid hit a rock and fell into the water. I took a wrong turn and went up a mountain, and by the time we got back to the shore, the tide had trapped us. We hoisted the four-wheelers over rocks. We forged on. We were laughing so hard we were crying. What a greater day of fun that was than if everything had gone right.

The same thinking applies at sea. Fishermen must be natural gamblers and eternal optimists; otherwise we would live in fear of the unknown, of failure, of death and injury. As fishermen, we do not know what the next season portends. We can only get our gear together the best we can and be ready for what nature has in store. From our experience of disasters, hard winters, broken, burned, sunk, and adrift boats, hunger and sickness, and the need for grit that physical isolation demands, commercial Bering Sea fishermen know our place in a unique and very dangerous profession. Alone on the sea—as I am now—we may not survive, but we start with the premise, as do most Alaskans, that our own rock-ribbed self-sufficiency will see us through.

We keep our fishing gear and *Time Bandit* in Homer in the off-season. But before we were ready to set out to fish for crab last year, we had to gear *down* from a summer of tendering, which is the monotonous but profitable work of hauling other boats' catch of herring and salmon to the canneries. We offloaded trans-vac pumps and weight boxes, and once the boat was stripped, we gave *Time Bandit* some overdue TLC.

Time Bandit is a 298-ton, 113-foot house-aft boat with a beam 28 feet across and a hold capacity of 120,000 pounds for king crab and of 175,000 pounds for opilio. The boat is a Hillstrand family affair. Our dad designed her, and together with my brothers, we built her in dry dock in Coos Bay, Oregon, for about $1.6 million. Dad decided to name her after the eponymous Terry Gilliam movie fantasy about six dwarves in a time ripple who set out to get "stinking rich." I suppose Dad was wishful thinking about his sons.

The boat construction left us with plenty of time to get into trouble. Andy was the worst, which is usually not the case. I was arm wrestling with a man we met in Joe Tang's, which had become our hangout after we were kicked out of every other bar in Coos Bay (naturally, we called Joe's sexy daughter "Poon"). For a reason that only Andy can explain, he jumped on my arm-wrestling opponent and began to beat the crap out of him. Andy grabbed him around the neck and Joe tried to pull him off by the legs, but Andy would not let go. Finally the police stopped the fight. I guess Andy thought that the man had insulted me; Andy is my body-guard, as I am his. He can say anything to me, but if anyone else crosses me with even an evil look Andy will be all over him like a cheap three-piece suit.

When we finished *Time Bandit*'s construction, after nine months, Dad said to us, "Okay, boys, this is your boat now." He was not *giving* it to us. He was offering it for sale. But we had no savings. He demanded a 33 percent share of the boat off the top from what we would earn crab fishing and for salmon tendering; in return he would make the payments on what was owed of the capital costs of *Time Bandit*.

He asked us, "Okay, where's your fuel money?" Of course, we had none. "Where are you going to get it?" he asked. We started with a $50,000 loan. Dad assumed we would fail. He was never one for optimism where his boys were concerned; we rarely could do right. "You'll never make it," he told us, which made us want to work like hell to succeed. Over eight tough, lean years we split what was left between us brothers after we had paid Dad, the crew, and upkeep on the boat. We did not have much to show, but we had a boat and loved the life. Dad gave us no breaks. In fact, he gave us nothing for free. At the final tally, we paid him $1.7 million for *Time Bandit*. We paid him off in full.

What we had bought from him was an incredibly stable platform seaworthy nearly beyond nautical measure. *Time Bandit* was designed and built for work and only work. She has an elegant and shapely bow, but the rest of her is pedestrian and squat as a potato-eating peasant. We decided, since we were going to spend more than half our lives aboard, to give ourselves more creature comforts than are customarily found on boats in the Bering Sea fleet. *Time Bandit* has a four-man sauna in the forepeak, staterooms with queen-size beds, and two bathrooms, one en suite in the stateroom that Andy and I share as co-captains. Ours looks like a normal bathroom with a vanity and sink, a full-length bathtub with a shower, a regular toilet, and cabinets for towels, cleaning chemicals, and gear. Below, the crew's bathroom contains a full-size clothes washer and dryer and a stand-up shower. And in the galley, we installed a dishwasher, microwave, full oven and range, a large refrigerator, and a wide-screen TV for viewing hundreds of DVDs that we catalog in a drawer.

Last year, before the start of the season, we hoisted *Time Bandit* up on the grid in dry dock to have the barnacles blasted off her hull and a fresh coat of paint sprayed on. This past year, with stricter environmental laws, we did not paint her ourselves, and the cost skyrocketed. When the paint was dry, we bolted new zincs to her keel to help preserve her bottom from rust. We repaired and refurbished her interior, replacing cabinets, carpets, the microwave, and the seat cushions, and we patched a square hole in a door where a massive rogue wave had flung the microwave off its bolts across the crew quarters and through the door. The same rogue ripped the oven and range unit off its moorings and skidded the refrigerator from one wall to another.

In late August, we tore down *Bandit*'s two 425-horsepower main Cummings engines, checked and adjusted the valves, and replaced filters. Each of the boat's four engines—two main and two auxiliaries—has separate fuel lines and filters for safety. Our brother Neal, who operates the hydraulics on deck with the grace and precision of a puppeteer when we are fishing for crab, also serves as *Time Bandit*'s engineer. He is constantly belowdecks running his hands over the engines, listening to them, and feeling their pulse. They are the heart of the boat, and without them, we would be at even greater risk on the Bering Sea in winter.

As we do before each new season, we prepared for the worst that the Bering Sea can give. We repacked the life rafts, two Satellite 406 EPRIBs, life rings, and life jackets and checked the integrity and check-by dates of our $800 survival suits. We nearly obsess over these with good reason: The many stories of how these suits of 3mm-thick neoprene have saved countless lives in the Bering Sea justify our attention. We upgrade with newer suits every couple of years and last year only added new strobe lights to the ones we already had. Next, we restocked our first aid kits. The Coastal Pilot that tells mariners where boats can transit had to be updated with new locations of buoys and navigational lights.

We take fire at sea, and sometimes fires at the dock, seriously. Not even a hole in the hull can sink a boat faster than a fire. We take the extinguishers to Eagle Safety for inspection every year. We carry twenty-four of them—four in the engine room, one in each stateroom, one in the forepeak, and two in the wheelhouse.

Not long ago, a fire onboard *Time Bandit* underscored the value of working extinguishers. At the time a crewman came back from town drunk; he was smoking a cigarette in the stateroom, someone complained, and a fight started. The cigarette in his hand landed in a pile of clothes. A half hour after the fight— and by then the crew had returned to town—I smelled smoke. I opened the stateroom door and flames roared out. A fire extinguisher emptied on the flames saved the boat. After that, I asked the crew to stop smoking in their stateroom. Besides, Andy, who does not smoke, hates the smell.

Andy and I once saved the crew off the *Princess Tamira*, which had a fire off the Barren Islands on a flat calm day. The engine was sucking water with the rear lazarette flooded, and water was popping out the exhaust tube, but despite everything, the *Tamira* refused to go down. The captain came on our boat. He did not want the *Tamira* to beach herself on the shore of the Barren Islands. He wanted her to sink in deep water in order to realize the insurance money. *Tamira* was going down but at her own slow pace. Her captain had named the boat after his daughter, and he was yelling at the boat, "Sink, you son of a bitch! Sink! You are as stubborn as my daughter. Sink!" Only at the last minute, *Tamira* did what she was told, stern first.

Another time, we *thought* we had a fire; Andy and I were crewmen on a boat named *Caprice.* We went to sleep, and sometime later a crewman awoke us, screaming "Fire!" We did't smell or see anything. The crewman ran to the wheelhouse, still yelling "Fire!" The captain pushed him aside to get downstairs with an extinguisher, yelling at us, "Where's the fire?" The crewman would not stop yelling "Fire! Fire!" We had no idea what was going on. It was then that we realized in our panic that we had never seen him before. He was not part of *Caprice's* crew. We asked him, "What fire?" He had no time to reply. He ran out on the deck. We followed him and watched him jump overboard. We assumed he was a nutcase, until we saw him race off in a Zodiac in the direction of a fishing boat that was lying about fifty yards off our starboard side, on fire. Its crew jumped into the sea in survival suits. We pulled them out, and together on the deck of *Caprice,* we watched their boat sink.

And there was a time when we were tied to the dock in Kodiak in front of the cannery. A purse seiner boat was moored with its stern nearly touching ours. Andy was conducting a fire drill on *Time Bandit*. In the middle of the drill one of our crewmen yelled "Fire!" I was looking around for smoke or flames.

"What fire?" I yelled back at him. I was freaking out. Black smoke rolled out of the purse seiner. We were not on fire. It was. We sprayed down their cabin with extinguishers. The flames spread. We needed saltwater, but the water was turned off on the dock. We ran a hose from the cannery instead and shoved it up the vent. About that time, we heard sirens in the distance. Trucks arrived, and an official in a white fireman's hat came up to the boat and angrily kicked our hose. He told us we were idiots and sent his men down in the cabin with re-breathers. Minutes later, they came out; the chief put the hose back where we had placed it, and Andy and I were going like, "First responders, yeah!" making fun of him.

Andy and I were on *Time Bandit* one time at the dock in Homer when a fire erupted in the oven. It was spreading fast. I grabbed an extinguisher, aimed it at the oven, and pulled the trigger: nothing happened. Andy looked through the window from the dock and yelled to me, "PULL the F U C K I N G pin." I thought I would burn to death. I was so excited I had forgotten to pull the safety pin. The third time he yelled, I heard him. I pulled the pin, and the extinguisher went *Whooooosshh*.

With as much time as we spend checking for safety, anyone would have reason to think that safety was always our first concern. But crab fishermen are famously independent. The truth be told, we resisted attempts at safety regulations that are compulsory in other industries. We did not want a faceless government telling us how to do our job. Our thinking was that if you could not figure out how to save your ass you should not go out there in the first place. In 1988, against our strident objections, Congress passed the first and only law aimed at improving the fishing industry's safety record. The Commercial Fishing Industry Vessel Safety Act mandated that boats carry life rafts, survival suits, and emergency beacons. But crab fishing on the Bering Sea remains the nation's most dangerous occupation. Once the new safety measures were in place, we liked them. And then we began to rely on them. Now we will not go fishing for crab on the Bering Sea without them.

In the final preparation stage, the work can be tedious. Last year while Neal and I worked on the boat, Andy shouldered the hard, miserable tasks of completing forms and other paperwork that one government agency or another require. He filled out Economic Development Reports (EDRs) indicating exactly how much crab we had caught the previous year and how much fuel *Time Bandit* had consumed. He applied to register and license *Time Bandit* and signed up with a crabbing co-op and for our Individual Fishing Quotas (IFQs) with the State of Alaska. The bureaucratic requirements seem endless and often bewildering. And while the reasoning behind the paperwork seems sound to me—to bring order out of chaos—it also seems excessive to fishermen and boat captains. My brother is not an accountant. Five or ten years ago we sent money to the state for a plastic king crab permit card. We jumped on a boat and went fishing. Now Andy has to contact our attorney, our accountant, and our co-op manager and make sure they have our paperwork, and only then do we go fishing.

Finally, we reloaded the deck. We hoisted onboard bin boards, which prevent the crab from being crushed in the holds, and crab pots, spare buoys, lines, baradai hoods, cod triggers, extra shots of line, door rubbers for the pots, hooks, hoppers, sorting tables, new crane lines, and rigging.

Bering Sea crabbers conceivably could do away with every other item of fishing equipment except for the pots and, of course, the boat. The pots weigh around 780 pounds and though they range in size, ours measure 7' x 8' x 32". Their frames are made of solid steel tubing covered with tough nylon webbing. Last year *Time Bandit* carried 137 pots on her deck. We moved them over to the *Bandit* on trailers from the cannery dock on the Spit and used our own crane to stack them. Then we rigged them. And finally, we repainted our numbers on the pot buoys and tagged each with the Alaska Fish & Game license authority.

Preparation, like what we do for *Bandit*, does not come cheap. A rebuilt main engine costs $60,000, and the *Bandit* has two.

Swapping out the motor costs $110,000. A normal paint job costs $100,000, with the sand blasting at $40,000 and paint at $60,000. New fire extinguishers cost $350 each and $100 to service, and a ten-man raft costs $2,000 to repack, times two. New pots cost $750, and with line the cost rises to $1,000, plus shipping, which is another $200. Red king crab and opilio bait costs $50,000. Diesel fuel costs $2.60/gallon and the tanks hold 20,000 gallons—or $52,000 for fuel that lasts a month. We pay $10,000 for groceries. Travel and lodging comes off the top. Boat and crew insurance costs $45,000 a year, and before we started pooling with our co-op it was $90,000.

In short, *Time Bandit* needs to gross $1 million before my brothers and I start to make money. My salary is roughly $4,000/month plus a crew share that averages $100,000-plus as a boat share if any money is left over. Outsiders think we are rolling in cash. But we ask ourselves, "You know how a crab fisherman makes a million bucks? He starts with two million."

Last, before leaving our base in Homer, we hire our crew. I do not take this process as seriously as I might, and Andy has to clean up my mistakes. That has earned him the nickname Axe Man. A crew properly chosen can make a fishing season. And we invest too much time, effort, and money in the season ahead to let deckhands determine our fate. We choose the best we can get. Unfortunately, the best at sea are not always the best on land. The crew who work best on deck are animals who should be dropped off at the sea buoys on the way to port; we could pick them up on the way out. They are only trouble on land and end up in fights and in jail. I want the animals. But I do not want to take care of them.

Not long ago, Bering Sea crewmen were a motley lot of

lowlifes mixed with a few of the best guys in the world. The work appealed to drifters and misfits and men running from the law, wives, alimony and child support payments, debt, addictions, and themselves. They looked for work on crab boats for fast money. They sought a quick way to get ahead so that they could start their ruined lives anew. They had nothing whatsoever to lose. They fought with their fists and complained and whined about the food, the work, and the weather. *Time Bandit* hired a crewman once who, never having worked on the Bering Sea, lived in a state of perpetual terror in the short time he was on the water. He was useless. Another young man told me after only a day at sea that either I agreed to take him back to Dutch Harbor or he was going to jump overboard, which I pointed out to him would be suicide. He did not care. I took him back. And last year, an African from Sudan jumped overboard in a calm sea. He had shaved his whole body the night before as if he were preparing for some sort of suicide ceremony. His life vest was found over in Beaver Inlet on the beach. His body was never found; either he made it ashore on Unalaska Island, or he drowned or died of hypothermia.

Add seasickness to everything else and a first-time crewman's work quickly turns to the worst misery. As a rule, we make even first-timers work through seasickness, which can strike down the biggest, strongest guy. I never know how a new crewman will work out until we are out in the middle of the Bering. One crewman of my choosing was seasick for three days. On the third day, with his pants wet and squishing in his boot, he told me, "I just filled my boot with pee."

I thought, "Oh, God!" I knew that his incontinence meant that his body was shutting down.

I told him to lie down in my wheelhouse stateroom. The sea was rough, but I think he was seasick because his mind was telling him to be seasick. He would have been seasick on a pond. I gave him pills to ease the symptoms. I called the Coast Guard flight surgeon in Kodiak on single sideband for advice. He told me on the radio to give the man Saltines and grape and apple juice. "Get the food in him even if it comes back up," he told me. He started peeing in his bed again. He came to the wheelhouse and told me, "I'm peeing orange foam." I took him straight back to Dutch. It took thirty-six hours and in that time, his body was shutting down from severe dehydration. He could not eat or drink. His liver was failing. He was shaking and pissing and puking and shitting on the floor. That was the worst case of sea-sickness I ever saw.

If a crewman gets seasick, more than likely we are already a day and a half out at sea. If he does not drink for a day and a half, he is in trouble. He will be in critical condition by the time he gets back to port, unless I can convince the Coast Guard to get him. But he would have to be dead for that.

We do not hire crewmen who have not fished before. There is usually a reason why a guy needs a job, because he is a piece of shit; these are the guys who come out and say, "I'm the best and baddest ass you ever had." I ask them, "Why don't you already have a job if you are the best and baddest guy who ever was? Every boat should want you."

My hiring techniques for crew often are left wanting. I will meet guys in bars who are looking for work. After a few shots of Crown Royal, I will offer them work. We throw back more shots. The new hire gets friendly. He thinks I am now his new best friend. He makes the mistake of gauging himself by me. I tell those guys, "Don't hang around me or you'll get fired."

Firing is where Axe Man comes in. He has dismissed eight or ten of my hires over the last few years. Lately, some real ding-a-lings have come aboard thanks to me. Last year I hired one crewman in a bar. I told him to be at the dock the next morning at seven. He showed up five hours late.

Andy asked him, "What are you doing here?"

He said, "Showing up for work." It was noon. "I was drunk with your brother."

Andy told him, "Yeah, but my brother was here working at seven."

He said, "Well, he won't fire me."

Andy said, "He already did, dude."

One guy I hired was arrested and thrown in jail on an outstanding felony warrant before he reached the boat. He was wanted for spousal abuse. The court had ordered him to stay no fewer than 150 feet away from his erstwhile girlfriend. The judge who had granted him bail told him, "I want to remind you what you did to this lady," and showed him photographs of a woman with raccoon eyes and a swollen face with deep purple bruises. The judge was pissed off. The guy defended himself, arguing that he and this girlfriend had been drunk and were fighting as usual. But he should have known that there is no excuse for hitting a chick.

We paid his bail and while we were driving back to the dock, he tried to explain his felony to me, and I told him to just shut up. Onboard, to keep him in mind of what he had done to his girlfriend, I put stickers on the corkboard, "No excuse for abuse." We gave him a hard time. While we were offloading our holds at the processor, he called his girlfriend, the same one he had beaten up and the judge had ordered him not to contact. We went out again for opilio, and he drank a bottle of booze and was shit-house drunk while working the deck, which is dangerous to do sober. I told him to throw the hook, and he fell over. I ordered him to move away from the rail, and he fell on his ass a second time. I told him to stay in his stateroom until he was sober, and he started to have seizures. He pissed himself and was shaking and doing the fish flop on the bed. I asked him what was wrong, and he said he had epilepsy—a "mild case," he added.

I said, "Trust me. It's not that mild. Where are your pills?"

He said, "I don't have any."

I pointed out that we were 350 miles from Dutch Harbor. He told me how his epilepsy came about. He was snorting cocaine with some guy in port when the guy shot him in the mouth with a .22 and the bullet lodged in his spine. The surgeons could not remove the bullet without killing him. The Axe Man told him, "You are GONE."

Some crewmen remind me of Homer Simpson repeating the same dumb behavior over and over again. Once on *Time Bandit* I told a crewman to change the air filter on one of our auxiliary engines. While he was down in the engine room, he thought he would put his hand over the turbo, which sucked his hand down its throat and chopped off the middle finger of his right hand. He came up to the wheelhouse dripping blood and said, "Dude, I cut my finger off." The turbo had shot his finger through the engine and out again. I put the finger part in a Baggie and stored it in the cold-cuts drawer of the fridge. When we reached Cold Bay late at night, before leaving the boat for the hospital, I put a hot dog in a Baggie. I told the guy, "Here's your finger. Now don't lose your finger." I had his finger in my pocket. At the hospital, he rolled out the Baggie.

He asked, "Doc, can you put this back on?" He was feeling sorry for himself.

The doctor said, "I don't know. This looks like a hot dog."

Andy and I went back to the boat. The finger was way past reattaching and the doctor pitched it, along with the wiener, in the garbage. The crewman got shit-house drunk and told the doctor to fuck off and never went in again for treatment. We went out fishing. On the seventh day, another crewman who had given Hot Dog Finger a hard time for chopping off his finger in the turbo chopped the same finger off his hand in the bait chopper. We had to take him back to the same doctor. She went, "You made him stay out for seven days with no finger?"

I said, "No, this is a second guy."

She did not understand.

We have a crewman, on and off, named Eddie, whom we call Pineapple Head, because he is Hawaiian. One year Eddie broke his ankle while we were all out fishing the Bering. He said it hurt but "pain didn't bother" him. After a week or so went by I took him to the clinic in Dutch Harbor, where the doctor put his leg in a plaster cast. That night Eddie was feeling constrained. And his leg itched. He slammed down several drinks. Slowly at first, he tore off the cast with his hands. And he scratched his leg with a sigh. Leaving the shards behind, when he got up to leave the bar he was weaving, either from the booze or the absent cast. At the time, no one thought to ask him which.

Some crewmen can be rough and difficult to deal with, and the captain must respond to insubordination with severe measures, like fists and guns. I keep an AK-47 aboard and zip-ties and 200-mph tape to restrain them. In one sense crabbing on the Bering Sea today is no different from when Captain Bligh ran the HMS *Bounty*. The captain must keep absolute authority over the crew. On *Time Bandit*, Andy and I are co-captains, which does not mean that we perform as captains at the same time. He is master of the boat in opilio season, and I take command when we fish for red king crab. Only one of us at a time has ultimate authority, which we never question between ourselves. The captain must be prepared to whip a crewman's ass or even his brother's ass when words fail to stop him.

Once I had to beat the shit out of two crewmen on another

boat when I was working as its captain. One of the crew was probably doing drugs, and he was pissing on the floor in his stateroom. I told him to knock it off. I came back a while later, and he had pissed on the floor again. This time I did not tell him to knock it off. I knocked him out. His buddy jumped me. It was a brawl in small spaces.

Over the years, I have seen the worst, from crewmen who are crystal-meth heads, thieves, dodgers who borrow money and do not pay it back, whiners who create bad morale among the crew, boozers and brawlers, shirkers and suicides-in-waiting. In crabbing, the order of the day can be the bottom of the barrel.

But I have also seen the best, and last year, with one exception, we had a crew I was proud of. For king crabs, Neal and Andy counted as crew. Neal handled the hydraulics and engineered the boat; Andy worked the deck. I was in charge. My knees hurt and my arms ache too much to work the deck anymore. So in opilio season, when Andy takes the captain's chair, we hire an additional deck crewman.

Joining us three Hillstrands last year was Shea Long, a friendly and eminently capable 24-year-old who one day will be a successful commercial fishing boat captain if he chooses. He reminds me of myself in my younger days. He told me, "I'm pretty stocked up on ways to kill myself." He skis with no regard for safety, snowboards, kayaks white water, and races motocross. The similarities end there. Shea does not drink or smoke and stays out of fights. He left Oregon State after a year of soaking up beer, girls, and parties. He went away to the sea until he decided what he wanted to do, and the sea hooked him. When he is working, Shea keeps his mouth shut, stays focused on work, and takes responsibility for more than himself. Last summer, while he was in charge of *Time Bandit* during the tendering season in Bristol Bay, he invited aboard a couple of wounded Army vets.

They amazed and humbled him. They told him that what he did was crazy and dangerous. He told them, "Don't be selling yourselves short. I do what I do. You *are* what you do. I've got my legs. Think of that. You think I'm crazy. But look at you! *That's* crazy."

Then there was Richard Gregoire, who comes from an old Homer family. Richard was born the same day as Hitler. This is worth mentioning. He is sweet natured, but if a seabird lands on deck, Richard can be ruthless. He has brought guns onboard and shoots birds in the rigging like he has a thing against birds. I figure his character trait has something to do with his birthday. Andy and I know and trust Richard. He has seen the worst of the sea. A tall young man with a strong back and a quiet cheerfulness, he tells new deckhands like Shea, "Have fun until it's serious, and when it's serious, get serious fast." He is a virtuoso at the Bering Sea Two-Step, the deck crewmen's shuffling dance that keeps them balanced in rough seas on deck.

Once, Richard burned down an island. We respect him for that. He and friends went camping on an island in a lake in Canada, north of Minnesota, and before turning in for the night, one of them went to take a shit in private. He was a conservationist. He lit a match to burn the toilet paper, which he covered over with dirt and detritus. Back at the campfire he quickly went to sleep. They were startled awake in the middle of the night by an inferno. Fires funneled over trees in great gouts of orange flame. They paddled their canoes off in haste and watched the whole island go up in smoke.

One afternoon last year over a meal, Richard was enumerating the girls he has screwed. He mentioned one name.

I said, "Oh, I had her, too."

Richard looked doubtful but hardly surprised. "You did?"

"In fact, she was my first love. Now she has three kids. I owe her husband a drink chip or a beer."

"Oh," Richard said, stumped for something to say.

We also hired Russell Newberry, who we can find when he goes missing on the boat in the forepeak sauna. Russell loves the steam. The crew calls him InSauna bin Russell. He is another Homerite about my age and a friend with an easy, engaging smile, an extended Fu Manchu, a quick mind, and almost as many opinions as me. He has a booming voice. Once I was watching a Seattle Mariners game on TV and amid all that pandemonium I heard Russell chanting "Ed . . . gar . . . Ed . . . gar," for Edgar Martinez, the team's great designated hitter. I sat up. I dialed his cell phone number. He was *at the game*. Russell has no ambition to be a crab boat captain. He does not want the stress. He is content, or as content as Russell can ever be, with working on deck in winters on the Bering Sea and taking charge of his own boat each July, gillnetting sockeye out of the Cook Inlet.

For the January opilio season, we took on a last crewman whom we quickly named Caveman. "Even a caveman can do it." For him, we had to keep the tasks simple. We did not know this when we signed him on. We hardly knew about him at all. We learned in a few hours that he liked to sleep. We had only seen him awake when he walked on the boat.

When a crew works well together, work looks easy. Rhythm and smoothness within a team of men working toward the same end can be a beautiful thing. On a crab deck, a new and inexperienced crewman generally will make extra work for himself and for others. But by watching the more seasoned crewmen, he will soon find a system or a method that minimizes the steps, and he starts to make the time count. Some in the crew never quite get there. They are awkward. They will not take criticism in the spirit of cooperation, and they quit, or Axe Man fires them. These same fishermen for some odd reason are always demanding respect from other crewmen. Demand respect? On a Bering Sea fishing boat, respect is strictly earned.

A crewman once came up to me and whined, "I put on my pants one leg at a time just like they do."

I told him, "Yeah, but they had their pants on one leg at a time four hours ago while you were still sleeping."

For many obvious reasons, crab fishing is like the military. The strongest guy in the world is of little use if he cannot do his job. You do not realize how far you can push your body until you fish for crab. It is worse than boot camp in the Marines. Some do it, and some don't. A little skinny guy with heart will beat a big strong guy with none. Imagine yourself with jellyfish stinging your face in the cold and loud and wet, and every muscle in your body hurts, and one guy says, "My arms hurt." You do not want to hear that shit. You *never* quit. And you will be amazed at what you can do. At sea the crew is a team. Two crewmen are physically unable to pull all the pots in a string. Andy and I have tried, and we worked until physical exhaustion took us off the deck. Yet Andy once showed himself to be a Superman. He personally pulled seven pots in an hour. I was in the wheelhouse at the time. I could see him down on the deck doing the work of five men—he ran the crane, pulled and stacked the pots, and sorted the crab. Andy has never been afraid of hard work, and neither have I. He will not tolerate a crewman who is not a team player but is an All That loudmouth. He hands them their asses tied with a bow. Andy, who is a better judge of people than I am, always says, "You have to assume that a new crewman is no good; otherwise, any form of trust might get you killed."

After working thirty-six hours straight, tempers can flare even among good crews. One time I was working on the deck with Andy when another crewman split Andy's head open with a picking hook. Actually, he had thrown the hook at Andy's face. He was screaming mad about something real or perceived; we never found out. The steel hook flew right past Andy's face and swung out and back and hit him in the head. Another time a crewman wanted to stab another crewman with a knife over smoking cigarettes on the boat. They had been working on deck for a couple of days without sleep and were at their limit of exhaustion. He bloodied the other guy's nose with his palm and told him, "Outside right now. I'm going to beat your ass." He pulled a knife. Andy and I were going to let them go at it. Andy did not see the knife until they were on deck, and he told them, "Knock it off. Put the knife down." They did as they were told, but they could not work out their differences. We threw one off the boat soon after that and replaced him with a crewman named Clark Sparks, who stayed with us for eight years.

Clark and I fished off the East Coast together back in the 1980s. One day in summer, I was aboard my boat F/V *Canyon Enterprise* out of Gloucester, Massachusetts. Clark was in charge of another boat. We got our gear out; he hauled his trawl and I hauled mine. He was fishing out of sight of me about eighteen miles away. His crew called me on the single sideband. "Clark's gone! Clark's gone," they said. I thought they were kidding me. There was no way he could be gone. The sea was flat calm. I cut my line and charged over there, two hours away. The accident must have happened while he was working near the trawl, which pulled him overboard and down. When the crew pulled up the trawl they probably pulled his body apart. He had to have been busted up too bad to swim. That same day we had our memorial for him. We cooked a big dinner. We threw his plate overboard, and we took swigs off a bottle and threw it over. We said good-bye in our own way.

The Coast Guard searched for his body for two days and found nothing in the Gulf Stream. The water was 81 degrees. I looked for twelve hours after everybody else gave up. I would not accept that he was gone. If that happened to me, I would not want my friends to stop looking. I would want them to give me every benefit of the doubt. I found cardboard from his bait boxes floating on the sea. I knew he was near there. I felt his spirit when I reached a spot 200 miles out of Gloucester off George's Bank. Dolphins were swimming there. I felt him. I could not believe he was gone. He was like losing a brother. He had become family. I miss Clark.

When we are crab fishing, either for king or opilio, we are rarely out for more than two weeks at a time, and that is plenty for the crew. After grinding hard, they start to deflate in that time. Their bodies weaken and they need more sleep. They start to get weird. Their behavior alters for the worse. They get argumentative and flinty. Even the best of them change. It happens on every boat on every trip. I imagine that it happened with Christopher Columbus. As captain, I have to understand basic psychology; it's not that the weather is too bad or the temperature on deck is too cold. It's that psychologically the crew gets beaten down. And that is when mistakes are made and accidents happen.

As time goes along, crewmen can choose either to work as deckhands as a career or advance themselves to boat captains. Or they can fade away. Time does not work in their favor. After a few years, they think they know better than the captain. They want to make decisions. But they are not the captains. Andy tells them, before they get too big for their britches, "The only job where you can start on top is a ditch digger. You're the head honcho from the start. Everything else, you have to work your way up, and if you have no desire for improvement, you will stay where you are, with your mouth shut." Some deckhands remain simple tools who will never get anywhere. Andy and I tell a joke about them: "What is long and hard on a crab fisherman? The second year of third grade." And we tell another one about the crewman who entered a bar with a ship's propeller sticking out of his ass. The bartender points this out to him. The crewman says, "Aye. How do you think I got here? It be driving me nuts."

These days, I believe we are lucky to find anybody to work on the deck, much less good hands like Shea and Richard and Russell. Look what we ask of them: Work steadily without sleep for seventy-two hours in freezing temperatures with saltwater spray keeping you constantly wet. We expect them to perform tasks that would call for accuracy and economy of movement on land, and out on a heaving deck, they are balancing their bodies when all that another person could do is hold on for dear life. The demands are heavy. An ocean of death lies over the rails. The weather on the Bering Sea needs to be experienced to be believed. Time has no meaning. In day, the sun gives light; in night, sodium lamps, which we call "the Norwegian sun," light their violent universe. Work and more work means bodies strained by overuse, sore muscles, and shattered spirits. During breaks, the food can taste lousy and must be eaten quickly. The living conditions are basic. What is there to like about crab fishing, except the money?

And for this misery, *Time Bandit*'s five crewmen are paid 30 percent of what the boat earns, less a share for diesel oil, bait, and food. In the opilio season last year, our crewmen grossed $32,000 apiece for the work of a couple weeks. Few jobs pay as much in that short a time, but the men know that after they have suffered through what the Bering Sea throws at them, nothing is free.

The Only Easy Day
Was Yesterday

By the time Russell Newberry had chugged (at eight knots) back to Kasilof cannery dock after a day of sockeye fishing, unloaded his salmon, cleaned the boat and walked through the gloaming to the junkyard fishing camp, he was prepared for a night's revelry—booze, maybe somebody would bring a woman, jokes, some hot food, and laughter. He was getting into it, warming his hands over the oil-drum fire, lubricating himself with a Bud, with Dino Sutherland and some others like phantoms in the flickering light, when during a lull in conversation he thought to ask, "Has anyone seen Johnathan?"

"Johnathan? No," several of the fishing campers replied in unison.

Russell understood the men's apparent lack of concern. Johnathan was erratic. Unpredictable behavior was his only consistent feature, if anyone were to ask, though hardly anyone in camp would say so to his face. It was a shared characteristic; hardly anyone could ever predict what the captain of another boat might do. Things happened. The weather changed. An engine blew. Tides gripped a stalled boat, either shoving it toward home or out to sea. A collision with a log easily creased a hull and crippled a boat. As for a captain not responding to radio calls, it happened all the time. Captains who are not catching fish the way other boats were reporting simply did not want to hear about their good fortune and snapped off the radio. Besides, who was to say Johnathan was even planning to return to Kasilof? Russell expected him, but so what? He was a professional fisherman capable of watching his own back.

But Johnathan was usually the first into Kasilof. And now that Russell had mentioned it, the men looked at one another like boys whose mother had caught them in a lie. Music was blasting from CD players in two parked pickup trucks with open doors. On a fold-out banquet table over by a derelict house trailer someone had laid out in foil pans a dinner of soggy macaroni and cheese and a salad that looked toxic. The food was cold and the booze bottles were a quarter empty.

"Has anyone heard from him *at all* today?" Russell asked

"Not since last night," Dino said.

Russell speed dialed Johnathan's cell phone number, then switched off his phone, remembering how Johnathan had fried his Razr last night on the fire.

"Maybe he went to Homer," Dino said. Along with Russell, Dino was Johnathan's oldest friend. "You know John. . . ."

Russell did know him. He knew that he would be the last person to miss another rowdy night in the Kasilof camp. "What was he going to do with his fish in Homer?"

"Russ, I didn't think of that."

"Did you talk to him today?"

"I just said not since last night," Dino said.

"Me, neither."

"You know Johnathan." Dino waited a minute. "I thought he hit El Dorado and didn't want us to know. I tried to reach him."

"He went out alone, didn't he?"

"Yes, he did."

Russell knew Johnathan especially well and for the longest time "because of the salmon thing." They both owned salmon boats, were original members of the Kasilof fishing camp, and loved sockeye for the immediacy of the catch. They deployed the gill net and minutes later knew what they had caught. No waiting. No boredom. Russell and Johnathan shared a common view of the fishing life: Everybody has a good time; easy come easy go; no matter what happens, there will always be another day of fishing. Russell often summed up his view of life by saying, "It would just kill me to leave this planet with a full tank of gas in the truck. You can just as easily get killed making a left hand turn in town as you can drown out on the Bering Sea; you *must* live today like it's your last; and the only easy day was yesterday."

As a teenager, he hung out with the Hillstrand brothers and was in and out of trouble because of them; the Hillstrand boys were always doing something that was on the edge, and their reputation in Homer in the summers was legendary. Russell was drawn to the sea because of his father, who had served in the Coast Guard in Kodiak, but Russell had to fight to find jobs as a teenager, while the Hillstrand brothers automatically went fishing with their father. The opportunity to work on *Time Bandit* had arisen a couple of times, but Russell chose other options on bigger and different boats each Bering Sea crab season, until recently, when he hired on with Johnathan and Andy as a crewmate.

The Kasilof camp brought them together with more leisure time than on the Bering Sea. The camp was all about camaraderie. They never knew when the salmon were going to come in to spawn. The men in the camp were set up to go when the fish arrived offshore. But until that moment, they waited only yards from the shore. And around an oil-drum fire, they talked about how much money they were going to make, about gear, women, and fishing in seasons past. Then suddenly, the fish were running. The men dashed for their boats. They went out and fished, and when they came back at the end of the day, as it was growing dark, they talked about where they had fished and what they had caught. Russell wanted to catch every single fish in the sea. That was his dream. He was so competitive. If he played tiddledywinks, he wanted to win each game.

If there were a camp hierarchy, Johnathan was the alpha dog. In the eyes of the other men, he was a pirate outlaw and a good fisherman who preferred to be lucky rather than good. He caught what he was fishing for, with the needed mindset to think like a fish. He had an unusual sense about which direction the fish were moving. He knew how to read the weather. The currents were no mystery to him.

Another trait the men admired about him was that he told them what he thought, right now. He would never talk about anyone behind their back. He talked about people straight up. If he liked you, he stared you in the eye and said so. And he was fun to be around, always laughing, even when the fish were going to other boats. Losing disappointed him but did not bring him down. He often told the younger men in camp, "Do you know what it means when guys like us get off to a bad start fishing? Not a damn thing."

Russell always said, "He'd give you the shirt off his back if he liked you. Hell, he'd give you everything except his cowboy boots, and I'm not sure I'd want to put *them* on."

Russell did not share Johnathan's propensity to fight. "He absolutely goes to it. I've seen him. He tries to avoid a fight. And when he can't, he turns into something that is very ugly. You stay the hell out of his way." Russell said.

But he trusted Johnathan with his life.

It was seven o'clock in the morning on the Bering Sea two years ago. Johnathan, serving as the captain of the *Debra D*, was in the wheelhouse figuring out where he wanted to look for crabs, while the crew, including Russell, were resting below in the knowledge that in another few hours they were going to be up working for three or four days straight. Russell was in his bunk. The boat rolled to starboard 30 degrees, back and forth, with the heavy seas. At one extreme, he would be nearly standing up in his bunk, then back down so that he was nearly standing on his head. Russell felt safe with Johnathan in the wheelhouse. Even when he was off duty and asleep in his stateroom, Johnathan would wake up every couple of hours to smoke a few cigarettes and would check the boat. He could feel the boat; he sensed small changes in his subconscious mind, like a slight change in the engine's rpms. He would smoke only three cigarettes and go back to bed.

Suddenly the boat rolled and did not come back. Russell jumped out of bed and ran up the stairs to the wheelhouse. He had one foot on the stairs and one on the bulkhead at the top of the stairs. He stuck his head up and looked across at Johnathan in the wheelhouse chair.

"Wow," Johnathan said. "I've never seen the boat do this before."

Russell thought, That's not what you want to hear the skipper say.

He ran below for his survival suit. The boat was laid over on its side and was not recovering. In a calm voice Johnathan ordered Russell and the crew to take their survival suits with them down to the deck and find out what was causing this catastrophic list. The minute they reached the deck, they saw that a rogue wave had slammed the boat and unshackled 10,000 pounds of frozen cod hanging bait, shoving it from the starboard side, where it was counterweighted by fuel oil tanks, to the port side.

"John told us what to do," said Russell.

They swung two crab pots over port side with the crane. The starboard rail was under water and the pots acted as outriggers, shifting enough weight to bring the boat back to only a 20-degree list, which enabled the crew to sort the bait and move the pots around to bring the boat back to an even keel.

But they were not out of trouble. They were in twenty-foot waves. The crane was sticking over port side, and another rogue wave could have wrapped the crane boom around the wheelhouse. The crew moved the bait—the hardest and fastest work they had done in their lives. Russell believed that Johnathan had saved their lives. "He was cool as a cucumber. He cracked jokes and kept up our morale as this was going on. He was constantly telling us that we were going to be all right. He did not panic once. On the other hand, I was a bucket of shit. I thought this was the end and wanted to get the life raft out right now."

Back at fishing camp an hour went by without hearing from Johnathan. Russell had a feeling in the pit of his stomach that something more was involved in Johnathan's delay; any easy excuse or explanation did not ring true. He paid attention to his sixth sense. Over a lifetime it had rarely betrayed him. He knew what he had to do. He did not know the best way to go about it. He could notify the Coast Guard, ask them to take a look. It was mid evening by now and growing dark in the Alaskan twilight. He could not have sat on the dock. Waiting was not his style. The Coast Guard might begin to search in daylight but Russell was not going to hang around for them to get started in the morning.

He asked Dino for his boat, *Rivers End* (or what the men in the camp called *Livers End*) to take a look for himself. Dino's boat could make 20 knots; Dino would want to go with him. But Russell wanted to go alone. It was better that way. He decided not to ask him, but just take his boat.

He reached into a trailer for a hooded sweatshirt and a slicker. He walked a couple hundred yards to the cannery's loading dock on the river. The tide was going out. An early rising half moon pushed up from the horizon. The mud-bottomed river flowed twenty feet below the dock. Slimers with billowy hair nets under their caps and rubber aprons leaned against stainless steel tables heading and gutting sockeye with sharp knives and sliding their bodies down a slick ramp where they were being packed in bins under ice; the salmon would leave the dock by truck for a processing plant that would flash freeze the fish before being flown overnight to Tokyo. The workers quietly concentrated on the speed of their knives and the nozzles that washed away the slime. The fish gleamed like chrome in the glare of sodium lights.

Almost as an afterthought, but knowing how close Johnathan and Andy were as brothers—Andy was the first person whom Johnathan called on the single sideband radio to ask him advice when the *Debra D* nearly capsized, and Andy, who was in the general area at the time, threw the throttles to the firewall to get *Time Bandit* over to the *Debra D* as fast as possible in case his brother needed to be rescued—Russell decided to call Andy and tell him. He checked his wristwatch for the three-hour time difference. And he dialed. Andy's wife, Sabrina, answered, and Russell exchanged pleasantries but he had an edge in his voice he could not hide. When Andy came on, he told him. Andy breathed out a long sigh. Russell could imagine him scratching his head. He had experienced this before, probably many times, with Johnathan getting into trouble. He asked what Russell planned to do, saying, "I can't get there, Russ. You'll have to shoulder this yourself."

"Yeah, I know," said Russell. "I just thought you'd want to know."

"I do. By the time I get there he'll be found or . . ."

"I'll find out what happened," said Russell.

"Call me one way or another every couple of hours," said Andy. "Good luck. And Russ? Thanks."

He Was Our Lodestone

Johnathan

I am still drifting on the *Fishing Fever*. But not like I was, and that could be a good sign. I may be in a slack tide, between flow and ebb. But tidal streams, currents, and the wind could be propelling me slowly to the southwest. Without a depth sounder, in the dark, I will not know if I am close to shore. I might have drifted out of the influence of tides in the Cook Inlet and into the Gulf of Alaska, where the rips are treacherous.

The wind has kicked up. The sky lowered in the last couple hours and is darkening now. A front is moving through from the north and west, where weather originates in this part of the world. One phenomenon that explains why the Bering Sea has the most unpredictable and violent storms on the planet, is that frigid weather fronts blow down from the Arctic as warm fronts press up from the Pacific. They collide on the north side of the Aleutian chain, which is the Bering Sea. The Shelikof Strait acts as a funnel for the winds generated by the monster fronts of the Pacific and Bering seas. Winds howl up the Strait off the land with a ferocious suction. For some reason, Alaskans call the winds Williwaws. They can blow 130 mph at their peak.

I never explain these natural phenomena to myself. I understood them once and forgot what I knew, intentionally, the better to ignore the danger. Just off Cape Douglas, currents from four directions meet—from the Kennedy Entrance, the Cook Inlet, the Kachemak Bay, and the Gulf of Alaska. The mountains behind Cape Douglas rise up from the sea in walls of ice and snow. It is a sight once seen you will never forget. The winds blow over the ice and snow and down on the waters below the Cape. It is 10 degrees colder there and winds blow 20 to 30 mph harder. The snow and ice become like tiny nicking blades against your skin. The waves, blown by the Williwaws, stack up in high and frequent sets. They build one against another, higher and higher. In a meteorological instant—as few as three or four hours—a fisherman can be in a fight for his life. The turbulence of the waters goes well beyond what any human who has not experienced it can imagine.

For something to do, I page through a book put out by the Alaska Fish & Game Department, which for some reason devotes several pages to the Beaufort Scale, which categorizes seas that fishermen can expect to experience in the Bering Sea. A Force 12 is the highest: "Sea is completely white with driving spray; winds are at 64 knots; visibility is very seriously affected; the air is filled with foam and spray." A Force 10 on the Beaufort Scale demonstrates the following weather: "Waves 29–41 feet, with very high waves with long overhanging crests; the resulting foam, in great patches, is blown in dense white streaks along the wind's direction; on the whole, sea surface takes a white appearance, bumbling of the sea is heavy and shock-like, with visibility affected." A Force 9 shows "winds of 41–47 knots with sea waves of 23–32 feet, with dense streaks of foam along the direction of the wind, and wave crests begin to topple, tumble, and roll over." For us on the Bering, while we have experienced Force 12 seas occasionally, and see Force 10 now and then, the routine for us is Force 8, which becomes a Force 9 or 10, and when a Force 11 happens, we are neither shocked nor surprised.

A ship went past in the far distance some time ago making about 30 knots northeast, toward either Anchorage or Kenai. I have a plastic signal-flare gun onboard, but I have not checked its condition; its shells are twelve years old. Some of my fishing camp buddies must be wondering why they have not heard from me. On other days when I am red salmon fishing, I check in from time to time to tell them what I am catching, and they must have assumed by now that I landed on hot fishing, that I am loading up and so busy I cannot talk on the radio. How would they know I do not have a working radio? We watch out for one another, but we are self-sufficient. We do not worry about friends. We know that they are capable, experienced hands who can get themselves out of most jams.

Earlier, I jumped down into the tank and chose a sockeye to eat for lunch. I had planned on a barbecue. Salmon can be eaten without adding another thing—no butter, no salt or spices, no nothing—and its juices taste great. This one was fat bellied, a female filled with roe. Her skin was slick and silvery. I held her in both hands. Back on the deck, I gutted and filleted her and set aside the roe. The meat was firm and bright red, a beautiful color that bears testimony to the wild open seas that salmon travel with vigor and enviable freedom.

I had the foresight yesterday to bring aboard a small bag of self-lighting charcoal, the kind you light a match with. I had wired a rusted, broken, three-legged Weber grill to the starboard rail in the stern out my way when I was picking salmon and cranking the reel. I lit the charcoal bag with my Bic. Flames erupted from the bag and nearly set my hair on fire. In only minutes I had a barbecue in the making and my mouth was watering. The charcoal was burning bright in blue flames fanned by the breezes of the Inlet. And then by accident I caught my boot on the Weber's leg, and the charcoal spilled over the deck. I quickly kicked the coals out a scupper. They hissed like angry snakes on the cold sea. I looked at the salmon fillets with yearning and put them back on ice.

With lunch a miss, I look through cabinets unopened in two years to discover a Sony shortwave radio under the instrument console. I find AA batteries and I search the dial for a weather station. As I tune the radio, I catch Dido's song, *White Flag,* with its refrain, "I will go down with this ship." I spook; she is a miserable quitter and a bad omen to a fisherman. No one goes down with the ship willingly, in advance, like she says she wants to do. You fight to your last breath to stay alive. Her message is a travesty. What kind of a signal does she send young people? Quit?

Truly, this coincidence of my situation and hearing this song freaks me out. I throw the radio overboard like it is a bomb. It will do me no good; I am at the mercy of nature that no radio announcement is going to change. I need another boat to come close enough to see me waving my arms. The only announcement that will do me a bit of good is a sign from another boat that it has seen me. My heart is pounding. I am glad the radio is gone. Weird occurrences like that have explanations, like a spirit from beyond trying to tell me something I don't want to hear.

That reminds me of the day our dad died. At the time, I was screwing a woman in a motel room, and suddenly, I could feel him in the room like his spirit was watching me. I quit what I was doing. I was embarrassed. The woman asked me what was wrong. I said nothing. I was thinking, *My dad died*. I did not learn about his death until the following day. I lay there staring at the ceiling. I truly believe in spirits. No one who works on the sea can help but have strong spiritual beliefs.

Sometimes, these take the form of superstitions, and I respect that. I feel small in the universe when I am at sea in an 80-knot blow. I am staring into the abyss. The edge of the earth is over the horizon. I have not yet gone off that edge, but I have seen it. I *know* my insignificance. I acknowledge that something out there unseen is much larger than me. And I live or I die according to the whim of that presence. That is all there really is. That is what the sea has taught me.

Dad died unexpectedly during a medical emergency flight from Homer to Anchorage. He had been fighting pneumonia. The news devastated my brothers and me. Andy and I visited his body at the funeral home in Homer. My stepmother did not allow the undertaker to embalm him. She is an environmentalist. The funeral director wanted to sell us a coffin for $15,000. We decided on the spot to build one. The director said, "I'll give you a piece of advice, young men. Most people, when they try to build a coffin, build it too small. That makes eternity uncomfortable for the dearly deceased. And the relatives end up coming in here and buying a coffin. You could save yourself the trouble. . . ."

We did not exactly build Dad a coffin, but we did not buy him one either. We built him a boat with a bow and a propeller and rope handles made of fishing line. We christened her *The Journey* and we designed her length at 6 foot 9 inch, which gave Dad plenty of legroom. We painted the "hull" black like the *Time Bandit*, and we wrote on the sides sayings like "Here's Johnny!" and signed our names. Building the coffin helped us to grieve and made us tighter as brothers. As we worked with saws and hammers, we told stories, like one in particular that made us laugh. It typified my dad. One day he was in the front yard fighting with a guy who was on top of him pounding away. Andy and I ran out of the house in our underwear to pull him off. I was carrying a baseball bat ready to kill the guy, but we separated them.

The guy was furious. "I'm going to call the cops on you."

My dad calmly told him, "You want their number?"

The guy looked suspiciously at Dad, who told him, "It's F-U-C-K Y-O-U."

I loved the old man. There was nobody like that guy.

Andy and I picked up his body at the morgue. He was lying on a table, and we froze at the sight of him lying there vulnerable, like he never was in life. I said, "OK, let's do what needs to be done." We dressed him in work clothes and a *Time Bandit* jacket and wrapped him in blankets. We drove his body home in my Chevy pickup. Before we nailed the lid shut on the coffin, we put in a can of Pabst Blue Ribbon beer, a Louis L'Amour paperback, a pack of Luckies, which had killed him, and notes that we wrote to him that we slipped into his pockets. A thousand people attended his wake, and nearly everybody cried. He could be generous and charming when he wanted to be, and people remembered his thoughtfulness.

The next day, we placed his casket aboard his boat *Bandit*, and with *Time Bandit* following in its wake, we sailed to the southern side of the Kachemak Bay, where Dad and my stepmother lived and where he asked to be interred. We dragged his coffin up the side of a hill, but before we could bury him, we had to dig a grave. We found an area of topsoil on the side of a cliff overlooking the water, but when we started digging we hit bedrock and his casket would not fit. My stepmother suggested a solution. She said, "I climbed over him many a night when he was passed out drunk, so just leave him there. It'll be like old times." Laughing and crying we finally buried him surrounded by solid rock with his head facing north.

Our old man was cut from a rough mold. His name was John Wesley Hillstrand. A fisherman through and through, he was tough, uncompromising, and profane. He worked as hard as he drank, and when he was drunk, he could be mean, but sober he was loving and even charismatic. With five young sons, he had his work cut out at home when he was not toiling on the sea.

We loved him. He was and, even now that he has passed away, is still our lodestone. As boys we thought he was fun to watch from a safe distance. For instance, at the fuel dock in Kodiak men looking for crew jobs would wait for Dad to bring in his seine boat. They knew from his reputation that he fired one or two deckhands after each trip, and by waiting for him to return to Kodiak, they could take their jobs. He fired fifty hands one summer on the same boat.

When his hat came off, man . . . it was like a signal flare lifting off in the air. We would laugh but never so that he could see us. One time he was screaming and cussing, probably at us, when a seagull flying by shit in his mouth. My brothers and I howled with laughter, and this once, he saw our point. As a perfectionist and a great fisherman, he saw black and white, with no gray. He would meet someone new and he would proclaim, "I don't like you," in three minutes if that was how he felt.

He owned the 91-foot *Sea Wife*, the 86-foot *Invader*, and both *Bandit* and *Time Bandit*, and he skippered them back when fishing on the Bering Sea went beyond dangerous. This was before boats were designed to carry tons of water in the middle crab tanks. In those days the Coast Guard did not look for crews of boats that sank. Boats went out on the Bering with no depth sounders, no EPIRBs, and no life rafts. (Dad was unusual in those days for carrying onboard his boats a twenty-four-man Northwest Airlines life raft.) For him not to have died before his time was a miracle.

Dad fished for shrimp, halibut, salmon, cod, and crab. They were all one catch to him, but he reserved a special place in his heart for king crab. Dad was confident in his abilities, but he was never flashy. He did what he did. Money to make a living motivated him, but his passion was fish. He liked being *the* guy who figured out what the fish were thinking. Filling up the boat was his joy. Men get fishing or they do not get it. Dad got it. Waiting for the next crab pot to rise to the surface drove him crazy with anticipation. He would tell us boys, "We have one reason to be alive, and that's to kill all the fish we can, and if you have a problem with that, if you don't want to work day and night to do it, you probably should get off this boat."

Once, when I was twelve or thirteen, Dad ordered Andy and me to put on "Gumby" survival suits on the beach at the end of the Spit. The Gumbys are constructed of thick red neoprene with feet and hands and a hood to protect men from a deadly cold sea. That day the wind was blowing up ten-foot waves off the Spit. The cold water would kill us in five or ten minutes without the Gumbys on. Dad ordered us to swim out to a skiff that was anchored a hundred yards offshore. The problem was, we could not swim in men's survival suits. We were boys. But we did as we were told. The waves threw us back on the beach. We fell in the water, and rocks pounded me on the head. I almost drowned trying to swim past the surf. The tide gripped Andy and pulled him farther out into the Bay toward open water. He panicked and was shouting for help. He thought he was going to drown. Dad was yelling at him, "Swim, you bastard! Swim!"

"I can't make it," Andy screamed back at him.

"Don't you ever quit, don't you ever quit!" Dad shouted.

"Come get me!" Andy shouted.

"No," said our dad. "Until you are dead, you never quit."

Tourists on the Spit who saw Andy's thrashings alerted the harbormaster who raced his skiff out to save Andy, who said that was the first time he was afraid of the sea.

Since that time, none of us Hillstrand boys ever quit—anything!

Dad taught me another hard lesson. My mother had already warned me about stealing. When I was five I stole a candy bar, and she made me take it back and apologize to the storeowner. Six years went by, and some kids stole one of our 25-horsepower Evinrude outboard engines. With what my brothers and I viewed as perfect logic, in turn I stole a pair of oars. It was only fair. My father was enraged when he found out. And I lied to him about it. He kicked my ass and shoved me out the door. "I didn't raise a family of liars or thieves," he shouted at my back. "You are no longer my son. You are *out* of the family." I was eleven. I slept overnight in a culvert in the freezing cold, as wet as a drowned rat. I went back home the next day because I had nowhere else to go and I was hungry.

Like it or not, he made us who we are.

Not long after my overnight in the culvert, I asked him how many beers would make me drunk, and he said, "Let's find out." He started drinking with me. It was cool getting drunk with your dad. The second time I was drunk, I downed a bottle of blackberry brandy. Dad was furious because he thought my friends had pressured me. He did not want his sons to be followers. For him, nuance and that moment's frame of mind meant everything. He did not mind that we grew pot out on the Spit. It was all the same to him, and we grew pot by the bagfuls. Grandma Jo sniffed out the plants, pulled them out by the roots, and took them to her house in her pickup truck and burned them in an oil-drum fire. We laughed imagining her standing by the drum, watching the flames, getting stoned.

Dad challenged us to make us better. He expected more of us. And yet he never refused us the freedom to be boys. My brothers and I were driving vans in town at ten and eleven years old. The Homer cop pulled us over and called our dad. Driving was a thrill, but Andy and I needed to find other things to go fast in. I went flying with friends with licenses, and I would hang out at the Homer airport and clean out lockers for free rides. If I had become a pilot, I would be dead now. I would have pushed the envelope too far, like I still do with motorcycles. When I was a teenager, I slid my first motorcycle under a Toyota. I raced motorcycles full throttle. I knew no other way. I drove my next bike, a street bike, through a stop sign at ninety at a T-bone intersection and went right under a car. Today, I own a Harley Fat Boy with a nitrous boost that generates 300 horsepower. I took the Harley out with a crabbing buddy, Phil Harris, who rides with no windscreen and no helmet. He was going ninety miles an hour down the highway lighting up one cigarette after another with a powerful butane lighter. That is what I call dedication. This spring I discharged the nitrous and was going 130 mph when I hit a turtle crossing the road. It scared the hell out of me but the rush cleared my mind of life's usual bullshit.

Like Andy says, "When we were five years old, Dad taught us everything about how to ride bikes except how to use the brakes." We thought of danger merely as a higher form of fun. A popular book today is titled *The Dangerous Book for Boys;* we did not need to read about danger. We lived it without knowing what it was; we knew how it felt, and it felt fine. Andy found a beehive one time that I wanted to set on fire. I was ready to douse it with a coffee can of gasoline, when he ran past me and slammed the hive with a two-by-four. Of course the bees buzzed after us. They could fly a whole lot faster than we could run, which surprised me at the time. And they were mad. We were running down the road pulling bees off our faces.

We also battled, nearly constantly, with rocks. We used garbage can lids for shields. We threw so many rocks at each other I think we changed the shape of the Spit. Inevitably, some rocks hit their targets. One summer, our mom was continually driving us to the Homer hospital's emergency room for stitches. On one visit, the doctor asked her, "Mrs. Hillstrand, you've seen this done enough times. Why don't *you* do it and save yourself the trip?"

We laid claim to my grandfather's old boat, *Try Again*, to play on. It was wrecked and listing on its side in the mud off the Spit, and we waded to it at low tide. When the tide flowed we were at sea covering continents in our dreams. We were *pirates*. With wooden swords, rocks, and garbage can lid shields, we ruled our imaginary world. We fended off anyone who dared to challenge our supremacy. Other boys liked to join our gang. Even as kids, we had reputations that worried mothers, especially mothers of girls, but our bad ways drew kids like drunks to an open bottle.

That reputation may have started when word got around that we had nearly drowned. Three of us, Andy, my youngest brother Neal, and I stole a twelve-foot, fiberglass, pumpkin seed sailboat that my dad had run over when someone parked it and two others like it illegally in his slip; the one that survived his rage had hairline cracks in its hull, and those cracks were soon our undoing.

We had spied the boat earlier in the morning, and as the day wore on, the thought of taking it for a joyride became irresistible. We talked about what our dad would do if he caught us, but the more we talked, the more certain we were that we would take the boat for a spin. It did not dawn on us that we did not know how to sail. And we set off. We were wearing jeans and T-shirts and baseball caps, and no life jackets. We pointed the bow in the direction of the other side of the bay, where we hung out in secret coves, sometimes camping for three or four nights at a time living off mussels, crow, squirrel, Dungeness crabs, and fish.

Two hundred yards off the Spit, the cracks started to leak, then gush water. The boat capsized. We were thrown out. We treaded freezing cold water. Our baseball hats floated away. We wanted to scream for help but we did not want anyone to find out that we had capsized the boat. Our true dilemma was the choice between drowning and dishonor. From the deck of the Land's End Inn our grandma had seen us tip over. We watched her run for help. We did not know how long we could hold out. Our body temperatures were dropping fast in 42-degree water. We were facing the Spit and just starting to panic, when a woman's voice rang out behind us. I turned around. There, twenty yards away, was our Sunday school teacher, out of the blue, going by us in her skiff, out for an afternoon of pleasure boating. She pulled us aboard, shivering and ragged wet, and with the capsized boat's painter tied to her boat's stern she towed the boat to shore as if nothing had happened. Like the stranger told me, one of the angels over my head was watching us that day.

Dad loved to hunt, which meant we hunted with him. We were younger than ten when he gave us our first guns— over-and-under .22s and .410s. Neal was into guns; he had taped shotgun shells to the end of his BB gun, using the BB as a firing pin. He had the most powerful BB gun in the world. He shot a raccoon with it. Neal, whom we called Diabolical and Neal the Eel, for carrying live eels in his pockets for snacks, had a hunger for combustibles. Once, he wondered what would happen if he threw a coffee can of gasoline on an open fire. The flame roared back at him. He spilled gas on his shirt and burst into flames. He ran around in circles, and we tackled him and rolled him in the dirt, but his burns sent him to the hospital anyway. Neal was always disappearing. He made himself scarce when Dad started yelling. He wandered quietly away. He fell out of the car on a trip to Buffalo. Neal once glued his eyes shut with super glue. He chopped down a tree that I was standing in. When he was fourteen, he hid in an arcade one night with a pillowcase and a crowbar. He jimmied open the vending machines and filled the case with $250 in quarters, which he dragged home, leaving a trail of quarters for six blocks. He would not say whether he won the money or had stolen it. We gave him the benefit of the doubt, but we knew the truth. We called him Diabolical because as boys we thought he possessed the greatest criminal mind of the last century.

Andy was cut from a similar pattern. He believed all dreams were possible. He wanted desperately to be an astronaut ever since he watched the moon landing on TV in sixth grade class. He built a rocket out of a zinc and tin garbage can. It was my idea to pack fireworks and explosive aerosols under the can as rocket booster propellants. Andy, with great ceremony and wearing his own version of a flight suit and helmet, climbed into the can. I lit the fuse. Andy never left the ground. But his trip to the emergency room was fast. One time, he fashioned wings out of balsa wood and newspapers, like a homemade kite, and attached them to his arms with string. He looked like a bat with headlines. We had our doubts, but the thought of him crashing was delicious. He climbed the tallest tree. He flapped his arms and jumped. There was no miracle that day, except that he did not kill himself. He only broke an arm.

We could beat up on each other. But if an outsider threatened us, Andy descended with fury. He has been there for us our whole lives, like the time I rolled a car off the Spit road. I did not want the police to revoke my license. I did not have insurance. I called Andy from the wreck site to come before the police arrived. In only minutes, without a question asked, he was greeting the authorities with a story that they did not believe but could not officially prove was a lie.

When Dad was away fishing, we used our guns without permission. We chose sides, and pitched battles began. We quickly learned to our delight that we were able to dodge .22 bullets from a quarter mile away. At Grandma's house we shot back and forth across an open field. To hear bullets snap overhead was cool. Fortunately, we were not good shots and no real danger to ourselves. For that, we had to wait until Dad took us mud duck hunting. Each time we returned to the skiff he ordered us to unload and hand off our guns for safety's sake. I handed up my gun to Andy and *boom*! It went off next to his head. He started to laugh. It was a psychotic laugh, like he was amazed to be alive. I did not have the same reaction when he shot me. I was standing in front of him when mud ducks flew toward us, and I said to myself, "He wouldn't shoot at them, would he?" He shot. The blast knocked me over. I picked myself up and picked pellets out of my rain gear right up my body to my face.

Oddly enough, Grandma Jo first taught us to shoot. We were eight or nine at the time, and she knew how the bears and moose frightened us when we visited the outhouse. She wanted to show us that she could protect us. Our grandfather Ernie had died by then and was buried in a grove near her homestead log house. He had killed two black bears from his front door with a .44 magnum pistol that he bequeathed Jo. While we watched, she drew the gun close to her face to aim and pulled the trigger. The recoil bucked the hammer into her head and gave her a mild concussion and powder burns.

Dad felt that killing a moose would somehow improve our character. One time I had just returned from a fishing trip and was tired. I had no desire to go hunting with my brothers and with Dad; to be honest, I had looked forward to a hotel with room service and a lady. But I went moose hunting. We flew to Emerald Lake and camped on the shore. The first day, Dad shot a moose, and I thought, *Hey, this is great. We can leave now.* The airplane came to pick us up. I was packed and ready. But then, the plane took off again without us. I could not believe my eyes. I said to Dad, "I thought we were leaving."

He said, "Not until everyone shoots a moose."

At that moment I saw a moose on a hill. I started running after it with my rifle, firing as I ran. I chased that damned animal until I could not stand up; at one point I nearly ran off a cliff. I was yelling at it I was so angry, and the more I yelled the faster it ran. The moose got away, and on that trip I never did bag a moose. Dad finally let us go home.

He organized these hunts down to the last pretzel. One time he brought along the sons of a friend. He planned out the stores, enough for each boy. There were seven oranges and seven apples and seven steaks, and so on. He put on the menu things I did not like, like liverwurst. I would rather eat moss and leaves. My brothers and I went for a hike with Dad, and while we were tromping around the mountains his friend's sons, whom we called the Cabelas Brothers (after the well-known outdoor outfitter) because of their spanky hunting outfits, ate *all* the oranges. The old man was beside himself. I thought, *there goes the hat.* He was so pissed off he kicked them out of camp.

We also hunted for the famous brown bears in Kodiak. One

time, as we neared the island on *Bandit*, a bear was swimming the Shelikof Strait twenty miles at sea from the direction of Ninagiak Island off Katmai National Monument toward Kodiak. The big animal looked beat; it tried to climb into our boat, and we went out of our way to avoid it. On that bear hunt, Andy got separated from us. We had no idea where to find him. He spent the night in a tree with brown bears prowling around under him. One time, when we were younger, Andy was sixty feet up in a tree with his gun waiting for a bear to walk by. We chopped down the tree, and Andy tried to fly again. He stuck out his tongue. And when he hit the ground, he nearly bit it off. Blood was everywhere.

My brothers and I started working on fishing boats when we were eight, and it could not have been too soon. I used to sit on the beach while Dad let me watch him sail out. I was mad about that. I wanted to work because I wanted to fish. Fishing is my oldest memory. I must have been two, and my brothers and I were aboard Dad's fishing boat. We were out with him doing what we could do, which was not much, but it was fishing anyway. Andy was crying in a bunk, and I tried to get to him to comfort him. My dad was running the boat. I reached Andy's bunk, and Dad told me, "I'm going to kill you if you don't get away from there." I could not see why he would not let me go over to Andy. But I did comfort him. After that, Dad kept me on land until I was eight. Out of the blue he told me one morning, "Come on, let's go fishing." That was my first working trip. As the bait boy I received one share of the catch, which meant $79 that my mother put in a savings account. I was suddenly rich beyond my imaginings. From then on, I worked for hours each day. If the fishing season was open, Andy and I fished. By the age of ten, I was working each summer with no time off. I did not know anything else. Dad said we were going fishing, and we loved it. We were like puppies. That was how fishing got in our blood. When we cut loose from Dad after we were teenagers, we looked around and we knew of nothing else with the same potential for fast money and such ample joy. Even at that tender age, we beat the older fishermen out on the fisheries. Our fish were bigger than their fish, and we caught more than they caught. That's what life was about. We competed through and through. Fishing hooked me entirely.

If we could not fish at sea, as boys, we fished off the Spit. The Kachemak Bay was out our back door. We caught fish, made a fire in the rocks, and baked it. And what remained of our catch we sold to the fish market in Homer for $1 a crab and $5 a salmon. One time with Dad and Mom's help we built a raft on the beach of scrap and driftwood. The finished craft weighed more than a battle tank. It sank to the bottom at the first launch. Dad felt sorry for us, I guess, because soon after he built us a hydroplane speedboat that looked sleek and dangerous, powered by two 50-horsepower Mercury engines. It was twelve feet long with a eighth-of-an-inch plywood hull. We drove with a recklessness that scared even him. He knew we would kill ourselves if we continued racing it, and he dug a hole with a backhoe and buried the boat. Even we understood why he did it. He told us, "I have given you boys every means at my disposal to kill yourselves, and you have failed."

We did not think about luck when we went fishing. We thought of fishing as catching fish. One time, as usual, tourists were throwing lines into the waters off the Spit, frustrated when no fish were biting. Homer promotes itself as "the halibut fishing capital of the world," and catching nothing does not conform to the ambitions of visitors who mob the Spit in the summers. Several men watched Andy and me throw a net into the water. They seemed to be amused by our boyish naïveté, I suppose. In no time, salmon filled our net. One guy slammed his pole down on the ground in disgust. Another time, we waited at midnight while visitors were combat fishing king salmon off the Spit in what we called "the fishing hole," a specific pool where the salmon returned each year. The town of Homer had decided to open this fishery at midnight. Watching the fishermen was fun. The men took it too seriously. They threw large sharp hooks into the pool in the hopes of snagging one of the frenzied fish, which would bite at anything that entered the water. They jerked back the lines with such violence that the hooks flew out of the salmons' mouths and planted themselves in the fishermen. The town fathers panicked over this carnage and from then on, stationed two ambulances at the ready by the pool. We threw a couple hooks, caught as many kings as we wanted, and walked off. The visitors hated us.

Boats were second nature to us. We learned to operate them starting with rowboats and skiffs and rafts. Older fishermen called us "skiff mice." We hot-rodded them, sank them, crashed them, and bought and sold them. We could do to boats what we would never be allowed to do to cars. There were no laws on the water then. To run the outboard engines, we needed to sit on a bucket to see over the bow. People on shore could see only our heads over the gunwales. We looked like five little monkeys in yellow rain gear cruising along offshore. Later, as we graduated to more powerful outboard motors, we terrorized the Inlet. One time, we were racing kids in another skiff, and Andy turned sharply. The 25-horsepower Evinrude outboard engine flew off our boat and sank out of sight. The other boat came back and hit a wave so hard, their engine split the transom, and it too dropped to the bottom. We laughed our way in to port, paddling with an oar. Dad was not happy.

The intensity of our younger lives, with this hunger for the joy of living, inevitably reached a pinnacle that included a world of pain. Andy and I liked to jump cars and motorcycles. I do not know why. I do not know the why of most things I used to do. Once we jumped a car so high we would have landed on the front bumper if a friend named Phil, who weighed 300 pounds, had not provided ballast in the backseat. He hurt his back permanently, and that was the last time he jumped with us. It was also the last time that particular car jumped or did anything else.

Andy bought a Honda CR80 bike that he jumped going 60 mph. When he landed, the handlebars dropped around the gas tank, and by all rights his neck should have snapped. A full-face helmet—the only time I ever saw him wear it—saved him. A friend ran over to him lying on the ground and said, "Man! That's the farthest I ever saw anyone jump in my life. Are you OK?" Andy was alive, but his spine was wrecked, and he could hardly walk. He had ruptured his spleen, hit his head, and broken ribs, and he was hallucinating when he picked himself off the ground. He could not breathe, and he said his life was flashing before his eyes. He saw sparks for days.

A few days later, I jumped off the *Frieda K*'s deck to the beach, which I thought was only five or so feet down from where I was standing. Maybe it was lower, but I was nineteen years old and thought of myself as immortal. Halfway down in midair I said to myself, "I should have landed by now." I fell twenty-eight feet to the beach. When I hit, my chin thumped between my feet and rocks flew off my chin. I broke both my ankles and my wrist. Numb with pain, I drove myself to a party, got laid, and only then went home. I said, "Andy, man, I have to go to the hospital." I do not know why I did not drive there myself, except I wanted to see how the pain went for a couple days on my own, like I did the time before, when my wrist was broken for a year, the bone became abscessed, and my body killed the bone. I just did not want to go to the hospital. Andy drove me to the emergency room. He was bent over like a little old man in pain and he dragged me along the corridor on my back by my one good arm. The nurses stared at us. "What the heck happened to you two?" they kept asking. They could not believe what they were seeing. The doctor told us, "You two just used up eight of your nine lives."

When they released me from the hospital, I lived in a supermarket shopping cart for six weeks. My brothers cut a hole in the bottom so that I could go to the toilet, and they pushed me around. I could move the cart myself with a stick like an oar. It was a miserable time. We went to a Night Ranger rock concert, with me in the cart. I was in the mosh pit in the cart. The group's guitarist, Brad Gillis, pointed at me from the stage and said, "Now *there's* a fan."

When I was twelve, our mother Joan called it quits with Dad. Their divorce might have contributed to our recklessness. But she had tolerated his ways long enough. He understood her point but was not willing to change. She told us, "He was something else, your father. He was a good fisherman though."

We moved with her like gypsies at first to Binghamton, New York, back to Homer, and then to Anchorage, and when she fell in love with Bob Phillips, who soon became our stepfather, we moved to Coeur d'Alene, Idaho, in the winters. Andy did not take well to the marriage news. We were riding in the station wagon when Bob and Mom told us about their plans. Andy jumped out the back window and ran up into the woods on the side of the road. It took a while for us to find him. To tell the truth, none of us took well to the news, and we reacted differently. My brother Dave started stuttering. With Andy, I developed an unspoken communication, like with an identical twin brother. Neal made himself scarcer. Michael, my next youngest brother, went into his own private world. We had only ourselves to depend on. We stuck together as brothers like never before.

In Idaho, Mom was religious and Bob was gentle. In Alaska, Dad was not religious; he was profane and he was rough. At home in Idaho, Mom would serve us dinner at the table; during summers in Alaska with Dad, we cooked steaks in the bow of the boat with a blowtorch. Bob tried to understand what we were going through. We were split between a mother and father who lived in two separate places and indeed, inhabited two different worlds. We had two homes and two sets of new parents, and we were uncertain which one loved us. In his way, Bob taught us to be men with solid, dependable natures that our father had never known even for himself. Bob was awesome. He had three of his own sons from a previous marriage, which made us a gang of eight boys in one house. Bob built a bike rack for ten bikes and nine motorcycles. In the house, we lived in a dormitory of bunk beds and dressers. Neighbors looked fretfully out their windows, terrified of what we planned next. We strung rope pulleys between trees. I swung from branch to branch in the tall trees like Tarzan. When we were not outside playing, we turned big appliance boxes into imaginary boats. We used our imaginations to the fullest. We were never bored. One time, when Mom came into the laundry room, we scattered but watched as she opened the dryer door. She jumped back and nearly had a heart attack. She let out a scream. And we were howling with laughter. Andy was going around and around in the dryer trying to break the family record of fifty-two spins without throwing up when he came out.

Outside in the winters, we picked the steepest hills to sled down and went skiing nearly every weekend.

One time, I told Bob, "Dad, I found a new trail. Follow me."

He asked, "Am I going to get killed?"

I told him, "No, there's just a little jump."

He followed me, and at the jump he went up in the air past the ski lift coming up the hill and almost landed in the lift chair. He told me he thought I was crazy.

Mom kept us busy. At her insistence, we took turns cleaning up the bathrooms and our bedrooms. We had a big house, with four bathrooms, but eight teenage boys would have made a crowd in a barracks. With Mom's approval, we raced soapbox cars that we made with our own hands. With Bob's encouragement, we skied with skill and daring. One winter we built an ice skating rink. We water skied in the late spring and early fall, raced motorcycles on ten acres of woodland, and on rainy days, played foosball in the basement. Sometimes, we framed houses with Bob to keep us busy with hammers and nails. Bob let us have guns and taught us to shoot pheasants with bows and arrows, and for practice he threw Frisbees in the air as targets. After we became somewhat proficient with the bows, he took us hunting. I would not allow my brothers to kill the birds, even if they could hit them with their arrows. I brought along a cage and a net, like I was fishing for pheasants. To be honest, I never liked killing. Once I shot a seagull that died a terrible death. I felt real bad. It was sick of me to do that.

I do not hunt anymore. I figure the equation like this: A seagull bites, kicks, and scratches to get by on the Bering Sea, and some guy like me comes along with a gun and *blam*! target practice. That seagull had a right to live. Even killing machines like sharks have a right, although I am not sensitive to ants. I cannot kill an octopus. It looks at you with those pleading eyes. I feel bad about killing herring. They are looking at you, man. Like 500,000 herrings in a net mean a million eyeballs looking at me, begging me to let them go free. I feel guilty. Maybe my mortality is whispering to me. The closer I get to dying, the more respect I have for life.

Andy was smart and a faster reader. Mom never had to tell him to do his homework; I did mine in school. Somehow, in spite of my plans and my temperament, I got my diploma. At graduation, when I went up to receive my parchment, the whole class cheered, I guess because they were amazed.

We kept secrets from Mom and Bob, like that we jumped off a railroad bridge into a lake, until one day, Neal took pictures of us. Mom saw the photos and was shocked by the height of the bridge compared to us in midair between the span and the water. The biggest secret we kept was what we did, and did not do, at school. I learned that I needed to write the first excuse note of the year in my own handwriting; every succeeding note I could then write myself when I wanted to play hooky. The counterfeit notes passed muster with the school principal, who compared the handwriting. I learned math by recalculating the number of days of school I could miss without being expelled. I was playing hooky in my senior year the day of our class picture; my classmates put a mannequin where I would have sat in the bleachers. It was not that I hated classes. I did not see the point. I knew what I wanted to do with my life. Each summer living with Dad proved in dollars and cents that fishing could be my living. Those teenage summer earnings ruined any thought of education beyond high school. At seventeen, I spent ten months on the ocean and made $128,000 back in the early 1980s. I bought three pickup trucks—and quickly totaled two of them. I did not invest or save. I did not pay taxes. I bought no land. I blew the money in one year without a sigh. With more money to be earned the next season, riches would never run out. As teenagers my brothers and I earned $12,000 in one summer working for Dad on his boat *Bold Ruler*—and $8,000 was a normal earning for us in the summers in the 1970s. I bought motorcycles, stereos, four-wheelers, cars, skis, clothes, and every one of our hearts' desires. I earned more than our teachers. I learned that money does not bring you happiness, but it buys you a new wet bike, and try not to smile when you are driving your wet bike! I had no sense of responsibility. I was going to fish my whole life. Why would I want a college education?

As for girlfriends, I was jaded before I knew the meaning of the word. I had chicks all over me because I was a new boy in Homer each summer, and I went back to Coeur d'Alene in the fall with my pockets bulging with cash. And in girls' minds I lived for adventure. We were like honey to bears. I dated several—girls, not bears—at once but kept them in the dark, as much as I was able. Strictly speaking, I did not date the type of girls who went to the proms or sat on the honor society. But in my senior year I decided to attend the prom. When I picked up my date, she walked down the stairs to greet me wearing a ball gown and high heels; she tripped on the hem and down came her strapless top, exposing a glorious view of her tits. At that moment, her mom and dad were preoccupied with the view out their front window of the Winnebago camper I had parked at the curb. Making matters much worse, and leaving nothing to their Christian imaginations, in front of the Winnebago on the lawn by the sidewalk two dogs were fucking like survival of their species depended on it. My prom night was over. Her father said no way. I did not argue.

Mom "saved" us in church. Or she tried to. We were raised religious. But I saw only hypocrisy. For a while, my brothers and I attended a Christian school in Coeur d'Alene, and those Christian girls, who talked the talk but did not walk the walk, had trouble keeping their panties on. The Christian schoolboys were as bad, smoking weed. I came out of my religious training, with apologies to Mom, being who I am. I made my own peace with God and do not push my beliefs on anyone. I do not care what people choose to believe: Seventy-two virgins in Heaven are fine with me if that is what Muslims hope for. All I ask of anyone: Please do not judge me.

Up or Down,
Broke or Flush

Johnathan

Earlier, before Dido sang her mournful "down with this ship," I was laughing with myself, naturally, about last season red salmon fishing on a day when I was scouting the water for jumpers, and I swerved *Fishing Fever* to avoid a huge log floating with the current. I slowed the boat to take a closer look. The log was posted. A metal sign with bullet holes nailed to its trunk warned, "No Trespassing. No Hunting. No Fishing."

Another year in the red salmon season, up near the Kenai River—there was no wind and the thermometer read about 80 degrees Fahrenheit—a million big black biting flies descended and blacked out the sun. I am talking biblical. I could not fish. They were Single White Black Flies Looking for Mates; they mistook my face for a mate. A fly swatter was not big enough. I needed a gun. I hid from them in the wheelhouse with the doors and windows shut. They tried to get in. I could not see through the glass. A forest fire apparently had forced them out of the woods, or the devil himself had shooed them over the water. I threw Clorox around the deck and shot the hose in the air. I told the crew, "I cannot work under these conditions," let go of my net, and hauled out about a mile to get free. When I came back my net was black with flies.

Not long afterward, I was salmon fishing near where I am drifting now. I was off Kodiak coming home from Sitka when I heard "MAYDAY! MAYDAY!" on the single sideband radio. The voice was weak. I thought the caller was using a handheld VHF radio. I asked what was their problem. "A man shot himself," I was told. "He shot himself in the hand." An hysterical woman's voice on the other end said, "He's in pain. He was fooling around with his gun."

The radio signal was weakening. I relayed her call to the Coast Guard in Kodiak. The injured man had blown his hand off intending to prove a wild theory about the safety of the gun's hammer. He did not think the gun would fire if he pressed the muzzle against his hand. He was bear hunting with his wife near Bear Mountain. Through my relay, the Coast Guard asked the woman about her husband's pain. On a scale of 1 to 10, what would she say it was? She said 15. The Coast Guard did not evacuate him from the beach. They used a helicopter and harness and plucked him out of the woods. With him flying to the Kodiak hospital, I started toward Homer, still twelve hours away. The Williwaws were whipping up the worst seas I had seen around Kodiak up to that time. The weather kicked my butt. The temperature turned bitter cold. The deck iced down. I was in forty-foot seas in icy conditions. I limped into Homer glad to be alive.

I wonder if I can repair the batteries just enough to get power off them to call on VHF. For the second time, I wedge myself down in the engine housing on the port side against the wall. I have no reserve power. This effort only serves to stain my clothes and hands and arms with grease. The reduction gear is junk, and the boat will not move under its own power. I crawl back out of the compartment and look to the north and west. The weather continues to deteriorate with a low from the north. I look for other boats, but other captains must be staying in harbor until this blow moves through. I ration my Winstons. I search for survival gear, just in case, and *mirabile dictu*! Rolled in a life jacket—I do not carry a survival suit on this boat—is a sealed bottle of Crown Royal for medicinal use. My getting drunk now is not going to help me into port. I light a cigarette and my stomach moans. I go out on the deck to the hold and reach down for the salmon I filleted for the barbecue. I place the filets on a cutting table on deck, and with a knife I slice into the salmon's thick red flanks. I eat the strips one by one, like sashimi. The Japanese, to whom most of the sockeye are shipped this time of year, would probably pay me for a place on *Fishing Fever*. I taste the wild goodness of the fresh salmon and smoke a cigarette and worry.

This drifting is not relaxing me. The quiet slap of waves makes me lonely. The sound helps me to sleep when I am safe, but it makes me jittery now. I am accustomed to the crash and boom of crabbing on the Bering Sea. An odd thought occurs to me: This is getting hairy. While I am fishing for either salmon or crabs I am always moving and reacting. I am thinking about crabs with barely a moment for reflection. Now I have nothing else to occupy me. Here, I just wait, passively, for someone to come along. I am alone, and I hate being alone. When alone, I think too much and for me that is dangerous. Survival is not at stake here, I tell myself. My eventual recovery is only a matter of time.

For a moment, I try to calculate the cost of this interruption. As a fisherman, in the best of times, I let the bills pile up on my desk. I pay my creditors at last, and the money is gone, until I start fishing again. Up and down, broke and flush. With this busted reduction gear, I will be in the hole $10,000 for repairs. I have $2,000 in fresh sockeye salmon in my tank. The season is only starting. If I can fix the engine and stay out for five weeks and can clear $10,000, the season will be a success despite this hiccup. In most seasons I make $20,000 off red salmon before I pay the IRS and fix the boat. That is not going to happen this year.

Twenty years ago, I learned the hard way that the Internal Revenue Service means business. As a young crab fisherman, back then, I neither paid withholding nor saved to pay the IRS at the end of the year. I was a kid. I would tell myself, "I'll pay the taxes the next trip," and never did. By the time I sobered up, the money was gone. On the next trip I forgot about saving. But the IRS did not hesitate to get in touch. I wound up owing them $130,000, with interest of, like, 3,000 percent per month. I was paying taxes on the money I earned to pay taxes. I was moving in reverse. I wrote a check for $6,000 and the next month I owed $130,000 all over again. I do not understand how this worked but it worked—for them! I declared federal bankruptcy when I was twenty-five. The government took my cars, motor-cycles, and a house. I paid them back over five years. And from then on, I shoved my assets, except for *Time Bandit*, which I own in partnership with three brothers, in the name of a woman from Homer I was living with. That may have sheltered the money from the IRS but it did not keep it from her. She left me with only my pickup truck. She was a woman scorned and not one iota more compassionate than the IRS. When we were dating, I put a tat of a wedding ring on my ring finger that says "Autumn," which is her name. For several years, I have whittled away at the tattoo with a knife to make it disappear under scar tissue.

The process has caused me pain. Sometimes I wake up at night to find myself trying to peel the tattoo off. It hurt going on, and it hurts coming off. You would be surprised how a tattoo can sink to the bone.

Morosely, I return to the wheelhouse and tuck myself up on the shelf and get back to the events of last year.

We said good-bye to Homer finally in mid-September. Waving to girlfriends and wives and other well-wishers, we steamed out of the harbor into the Kachemak Bay, heading toward the Aleutian Islands chain and the crab fishing base in Dutch Harbor on Unalaska. In those moments, everyone in the crew felt the thrill of another season. The summer was ending, tendering was behind *Time Bandit*, preparations had been thorough and complete, and now we were heading out to do what we love. Soon we would feel the pleasure of full pots, plugged fish holds, and the incomparable pride of knowing we had beaten the odds one more time. As Andy says with only a touch of melodrama, "We look over the abyss and we survive." We moved out of the Kachemak Bay and pointed our bow toward the north side of Kodiak Island.

The cold wind and spray hissing against the wheelhouse windows gave me an almost overwhelming joy of freedom. I had cast loose the immediate past, and out here on the sea, my "other" land-side life of girlfriends, debts, obligations, family and friends, worries, and children was behind me. Those I knew on land could not reach me where I was going. My mind was cleared. I was free as any man at any time anywhere on earth and I was about to do the thing I truly love: fish for crab on my own boat in an inhospitable sea. Other men work for the benefits or money or both. My idea of being rich is doing what I want. In life, I have a good deal. If I were to be gone tomorrow, I would have no complaints. I have lived the way I wanted to live. The exhilaration of crabbing in a new season, last year and every other year, was impossible to measure. It could only be felt deep within the heart.

The run out the Aleutian chain 750 miles from Homer to Dutch, past islands with Aleut names of Unga, Sanak, Sutwik, Unimak, and Akutan, and Russian names like Popov, Korovin, and Ivanof (that allude to the history of this long peninsula), took the better part of an uneventful week. We were excited to see Dutch Harbor again. Some undefined mystique about Unalaska and Dutch Harbor confirms that we have severed our connections with normal life. Dutch is like what the border towns in Mexico were once like, and maybe still are—places of complete abandon, implied risk and even danger, of the exotic and unfamiliar, a nearly fabled place committed to hard work and hard play, a place devoid of beauty or softness, and a launching pad into the unknown. In winter, Dutch is like being on a hard ship at sea.

We tied up in Dutch's outer harbor in a crowd of other boats with names like *Storm Petrel, Morning Star, Golden Alaska, Northeast Explorer, Chelsea K,* and *Aleutian Challenger.* As quickly as we could secure the lines to the dock, we were off on a visit to the world headquarters for crabbers, Latitudes, a bar of longstanding notoriety. Once known as the Elbow Room, "the second most dangerous place on earth," for the number and ferocity of the fights there, remnants of Latitudes's earlier incarnations can be found today in the fading purple paint under the flaking blue paint of a recent remodeling. Nothing like a sign of welcome marks Latitudes, but the crabbing fleet knows where to slake its thirst for alcohol and its hunger for companionship.

Latitudes is about the size of a doublewide trailer with cheap linoleum floors, a long scarred bar, and a stage, now a storage area, where Jimmy Buffet played a gig in his younger, less renowned years. Music now comes at ear-melting levels from a jukebox. The one false note in the décor, such as it is, is a large painting on a remote wall that depicts sailors drowning. It seems too unlikely to be true, but there it hangs. To protect the art from destruction from the likes of me—I hate this kind of reminder—the painting hangs behind a Plexiglas shield in a shadowed corner. Over by the bar, a ship's brass bell, with a clangor tied to a braided rope, signals drinks all around paid for by the one who rings the bell, who may have struck the mother lode of king crabs or may be drunk and generous.

People who do not know us wonder why crabbers in particular, and fishermen in general, drink as much as we do. I answer them honestly. If we did not get drunk when we came in from the Bering Sea we would not forget what we had just gone through and we would probably never go out again. We do not want to be sober in port, coming or going. We are about to leave for the sea on a boat with no women and indeed, no life to speak of. We will work. That is all we will do. And so we fortify ourselves against that imminent reality. And we meet friends in the bar and drink because that is what happens in bars. Drinking is a social activity, and if we sometimes get too social and get drunk, there is no excusing it. And all the explanations in the world never really hold up to reason.

The young women tending bar at Latitudes do not serve so much as push drinks in the nicest ways, with smiles and chatter; they listen to our tales sometimes as if they are even interested. They laugh, and they are women, which is often enough of an encouragement to keep us ordering drinks. Like the crabbers, the bartenders too must make money to last them a year in only weeks. A breed of adventurers every bit as dauntless as the crabbers, these young women handle the male bar clients with humor, cleavage, and sisterly affection. Lisa, the bartender at the Grand Aleutian, told me last year that she wondered whether her life's role "wasn't to take care of crabbers. These guys are the life—the soul, really—of this sea-based business and the link between the past and the present." She makes certain that a full shot glass appears before the last one is finished. Someone else pays, I pay, the bar pays—the economics mysteriously work out. The women bartenders love us partly because we throw money around like confetti. We believe that generosity and good cheer count as much as breathing. Here today and gone tomorrow, and the barmaids cheer that attitude. They see it nowhere else in this high a dosage.

Alaskans in general have a drinking problem. I handle my part of it. Growing up, locals called Homer a "quaint drinking village with a fishing problem." The same could be easily said of Dutch and a thousand other Alaskan villages. Maybe the dark winters, or the cold, contribute to this thirst for booze. Could it be explained at Latitudes that heat does not come from a furnace? Warmth pours from bottles of Crown Royal, cans of Budweiser, and from human bodies crammed together. While the once-famous, never-ending line that snaked across the potholed parking lot waiting to enter the Elbow Room is shorter now outside Latitudes, the bar has retained its soul, when the crabbers come to town.

Dutch, and its home island of Unalaska, has tried to change its well-earned Wild West image; prior to the 1960s the island had no image to boast of at all. It had history, which was hardly triumphant. The only land in North America, besides Pearl Harbor, that Japanese Zeros bombed during World War II, to this day U.S. Army bunkers, Quonset huts, and barracks dot Unalaska's green hills in summer. But the results of the conscious effort to upgrade Unalaska's image to date are decidedly mixed.

Twenty years ago, bankruptcy threatened the local government when Unalaska defaulted on loans to build an airport, which was eventually completed and counts now as an essential transportation hub, albeit one with the single most terrifying landing strip in the United States if not the world, with gale-force winds, ice, blowing snow, and a jagged rocky ledge yards away from wing tips. Airplanes approach from the sea or the harbor only yards off the end of the strip. An official airport pickup truck drives to the end of the landing field and blocks auto traffic before each airplane takes off on the chance that it will crash into cars and trucks driving to the docks. Flights not infrequently abort approaches because of rapidly changing weather and divert forty minutes away to Cold Bay's runway, which NASA maintains in pristine shape as an emergency strip for the space shuttle. There are always surprises flying into Dutch. Not long ago a woman sitting beside me, looking out the window, exclaimed, "My, what a big fish." I looked. "Lady, that's a humpback whale."

Civilization of sorts came to Unalaska a few years ago when the world's largest cannery, Unisea, built the Grand Aleutian Hotel with the Chart Room, its superb restaurant. After king crab season last year, the crew of the *Cornelia Marie* was in the restaurant at an adjoining table with the crew of *Time Bandit*, and through the meal we exchanged toasts, barbs, wisecracks, loud conversation, and stale jokes, like, "You know you're a crab fisherman when your wife changes her name to Sharon Peters." The chef in the Chart Room presided over an eight-foot table of desserts that he was rightfully proud of. Without much warning, a crewman from the *Cornelia Marie* started a food fight. Soon the air was thick with profiteroles, tiramisu, mousse au chocolat, and globs of homemade ice cream. The hotel security guards and the Unalaska constabulary arrived with their pistols and Tasers holstered. Restoring order, they seemed embarrassed for us, with our faces and hair covered with sticky sweets. The chef kicked out anyone in the room with frosting in his hair. That was most of us. The party continued in the downstairs bar, which was where we were going anyway.

That kind of official vigilance keeps the island less rowdy but it robs some of its soul. Such is progress. Latitudes is closing, which is yet another sign of the times. Last year, the Dutch police stopped me for driving *one* mile an hour over the speed limit of twenty-five in bright daylight. The deputy must have been new. I told her, "Ma'am, you have to be kidding." She told me to stay in the car. She said, "Sir, I am saving your life." I drove away with a ticket and a sinking feeling for the island.

As further evidence of changing times, the bars close at one a.m. And services on Sundays at the historical Holy Ascension Russian Orthodox church, with its beautiful blue onion domes and sturdy concrete walls to fend off icy blasts of wind, help to give the island a family feeling that is at once new and, among the crabbers, not altogether welcome. Most of the island's thirty miles of roads are paved, but then each year the hard winters reduce the surfaces to rock and rubble. I have the suspicion that rubble would be the fate of the long campaign to civilize Dutch if the crabbing fleet had not been forced to cope three years ago with epic changes, which had been a long time coming.

Until the 1970s, Russian and Japanese industrial fleets dominated the Alaskan crab fishery. When I was younger, out fishing with my dad, I remember seeing giant Russian ships scoop "red bags" of twenty to thirty tons of fish and crabs from our coastal waters. My dad and his generation could do nothing but stand by, watch, and lobby their congressmen. They were forced to fish for crab closer inshore. In 1973, for example, Russian ships took 2.2 billion pounds of fish and Japanese took 4.6 billion pounds from Alaskan waters, within the 200-mile limit, while Alaskan fishermen took only 1.4 billion pounds from the same waters. My father's generation stayed out of the Russians' way and remained all but strangers to the grounds in the Bering Sea. I listened to my dad complain that the Russians were depleting our stocks of fish and if they continued, fishing in Alaska would die. He felt personally about it. He bitched to anyone who would listen, and it was usually me. I grew to hate the Russians, and I dreamed of reprisals. It was the Cold War. They were twice my enemy, and I vowed to get even.

In the early 1990s, I finally had my chance. The Cold War was ending, but the Russian navy patrolled their side of the international border. Their boats were not raiding our waters anymore, but one day I fished their grounds, with what I decided would be a symbolic Cold War payback—*Time Bandit* vs. the Russian navy.

At the time, I was cruising eight nautical miles inside Russian waters, near the Siberian coast, dropping crab pots in thick fog, when out of the gray a battleship came straight at me. I honestly shit my pants. I am more foolhardy than I am brave, and this confrontation now required me to be brave on steroids. The Russians were paranoid. They probably thought *Time Bandit* was a spy ship but exactly what it was spying on would have been hard for even them to say. A couple years before, they had seized an American crabber in these same waters. The sad thing about that episode was that the American boat was not poaching Russian crabs like I was trying to. The crew had stopped for souvenir T-shirts on Little Diomedes Island three miles over the Russian line. The Russians locked up the crew, brought them to their mainland, tried them *naked* in court, convicted them, and only after months of diplomacy, released them. The Russians impounded their boat, which remains in Russia to this day. I knew the risks I was taking. But I was not worried, until I saw the battleship *Potemkin* headed my way.

In those years, the Global Positioning System (GPS) was a new technology that the U.S. Air Force did not make available to the public until 1993. Until it arrived on the scene I rarely bothered taking longitude and latitude fixes while out fishing in the Bering Sea. I knew our locations out of habit, and *Time Bandit*'s compass guided me. I knew where to find the best opilio crab grounds. I cared about nothing else.

On the radio the Russians asked me to identify myself. They spoke in broken English, and I mumbled a reply in the hope they would not understand. I called the U.S. Coast Guard on single sideband. The Coasties sounded panicked when I told them. I wanted them to send Air Force jets to my rescue. But that would not be the Coast Guard. Their orders to me were very specific: "DO NOT STOP! DO NOT LET THEM BOARD YOU. KEEP COMING."

Apparently, my call stirred up an immediate commotion that reached back to Washington. Those waters were sensitive, I guessed later, mainly because the Air Force and U.S. Navy had a submarine and missile base on one of the farthest islands in the Aleutian chain, Adak, not that far from where I was dropping pots.

I told the Russians I would stop my engines as they had demanded, and of course I would wait for them to board us. And then, hanging up, I gunned it.

I do not know how fast *Time Bandit* was going, but that battleship was going faster. Those things move like speedboats. I calculated how much time I needed to cover the eight miles— about an hour, the longest sixty minutes of my life. *Time Bandit* crossed the line into American waters with the Russian warship about a quarter mile behind, and we aboard *Time Bandit* were high-fiving each other and shouting and jumping around on the deck like we had won the Cold War. The battleship slammed on its brakes, turned around, and headed back toward Little Diomedes. We waited until dark. As the hours went by, our radar showed five more warships, then nine, waiting for us to come back to retrieve the four crab pots we had left behind to soak.

Their boats moved north and south, up and down their side of the border, while we stood off several miles on our side. I think they figured out we would not leave our remaining pots behind. And if we came for them they would not let us get away again. I debated whether we should call it quits, but I decided no. I had to uphold the honor of the American flag, represented by those four American pots!

The crew voted for the raid. I had expected them to. But I did not influence their decision. In fact, they were excited, because part of the cost of those pots, if they were left behind, would come out of their pay. And that money could be better spent at Latitudes in Dutch. We made our plan.

We had dropped the pots a quarter mile apart. The deck crew can bring up a pot in three minutes. We needed forty-five minutes to reach the first pot, at least another fifteen minutes to pull them in, and a further forty-five minutes to get back over the line. The warships by now were nowhere on my radar. We were emboldened by the first escape, and besides, if the Russians saw us pulling pots they might change their minds about us being a spy boat. This, of course, was wishful thinking.

We ran up to the international border. We cruised parallel to the imaginary line by a couple hundred yards, until I reached a point that gave *Time Bandit* a direct shot to the first pot in the string. I turned ninety degrees to port and chugged across the international boundary, expecting to see the Russian armada on radar at any minute. We reached the first pot. The crew was ready at the block and the crane. They worked fast to haul it in. I brought *Time Bandit* up on the second pot, then the third. By now, I wondered if the Russians had given up. I was beginning to feel . . . well, almost relaxed. We approached our last pot, and the crew was about to throw the hook, when what looked like the entire Russian navy came up on the horizon. I pushed the throttles. On the loud hailer I told the crew to forget the last pot and come inside. Seeing the Russian navy, and assuming that they were watching us through binoculars, we gathered outside on the stern deck of *Time Bandit* and shot the Russians the bird and pulled down our pants and mooned them. I turned the boat east. The race was on. This time, the Russians did not try to radio us. They were coming to seize *Time Bandit*.

I imagined an engine frying, the steering going bad, a man overboard. Any problem now could spell our doom. The thought recurred of standing in a Russian court naked. The crew came in the wheelhouse to watch. We were yelling and screaming. We were losing ground to the Russians. Eventually, they would catch us. I did not have an exact fix on the boundary, but I knew the Russians would turn before they reached it. And turn they did. We cut our engines and more or less floated and gloated. It was a feeling of triumph at least as satisfying as returning home with plugged tanks of crabs.

I am aware, as is nearly every crab fisherman, that superstitions are created to give us the illusion of control over what we have no control over—the seas, the weather, the catch, the boat, and our mortality. Some of the beliefs seem stupid to me—like the one about bananas onboard a fishing vessel bringing bad luck.

But my attitude changed one day about ten years ago out in the Bering Sea when a long-winged glaucous gull, sleek and white with a "blood" spot on its yellow bill, hovered over my boat's stacks, I thought, like a harbinger of nothing good.

By all reason, the gull should not have been there. Sea birds fly over us all the time looking and waiting for scraps of bait, but they ground themselves on the sea when the wind blows 70 knots, like it was that day. The gull's appearance, when the other birds had settled on the sea, made me curious at first, and in the next moment gave me an uneasy feeling. Alone in the wheelhouse, and for no reason that I can think of, I recalled an ancient superstition that the soul of a drowned sailor departs his body only to be adopted by a hovering gull, like this one. The recollection gave me the shivers.

Flying with the wind, the gull sped past, and it could barely keep up with the eight knots we were making when it circled around. The seas in the Bering, as I have said, can be brutish. This day, the swells were rising around forty-five feet with some rogues coming in at sixty. I had to push the throttles to keep the boat straight into the oncoming wave, then relax the screws for the sleigh ride down into the trough, where all that I could see ahead was the mountain of the next wave rising almost impossibly, higher and higher, above the boat—a sight to make my knees quake—and behind, another mountain of a wave above the transom. The "money shot" in the *Perfect Storm* movie, when the boat climbs up the 100-foot wave and falls back to its doom, draws an exaggerated but nevertheless accurate picture. Cut that image in half and that was my day.

The Bering is a shallow sea, and the winds and currents churn the water up off a deep-water shelf along the sea bottom north and south of Little Diomedes, creating huge seas. Each cubic yard of water weighs 1,500 pounds, and a rogue, when it washes over our rails, dumps hundreds of cubic yards in one hammer-like blow against the deck. In a storm the sea swirls a boat in several unsettling directions at once, with the hull, stern, and bow each trying to accommodate the waves.

The Bering is a dark, ugly sea. The sky presses down on the water, gray upon gray, creating a morbid feeling of being trapped in a coffin in a storm. The grays of the Bering after a while form a palette of shades—blue bruise grays, black grays, light grays, green grays—until no gray is a good gray. Gray to me means weather, and the darker the shade the worse I expect from the sea. That day, I was holding on for my own safety, with my legs spread wide and one hand clutching a shelf and the other hand hard on the throttles. If I lost my balance, I would possibly fly across the interior of the wheelhouse, ending in a bruising collision with the port side bulkhead about twenty-five feet away.

The gull should have been sheltering either on the spindrift waves or on the desolate, treeless, and storm-blown Pribilof Islands about twenty-five miles to the west of us, and not that far from the Arctic ice pack and the Russian border. The bird had none of the usual reasons to follow us. I had called the crew in. One green-water wave over the bow and I quit. I got on the loud hailer and told them, "Okay, we're done, guys. Get off the deck." If I were ever responsible for a death in my crew, I would not be able to fish again. Even Maydays on the radios from other boats are almost too painful for me to stand. The decks were clean with no discarded gutted and bloodied cod or ground up herring discharge to attract gulls.

Most people may not know that these birds, especially the glaucous species, can be aggressive toward humans. Should a seaman fall overboard, gulls will immediately think he is discarded food and hover over him, darting and diving while trying to pluck the eyes from his head as if he were a salmon carcass. For a moment, the lonely bird landed on the deck and then rose to the height of the crane boom, as if it were impatient about something. It looked as miserable as an old man in a downpour, hunching its neck into its shoulders against the winds and the biting frozen spray.

The crew was holding on, watching DVDs, reading magazines to pass the time, fixing themselves snacks, doing what they do, talking, dozing, trying to keep their breakfasts down. Some were failing to do just that in *Time Bandit*'s two heads. We had been prospecting for crabs, throwing off pots to find where opilio crabs were roaming along the sea floor. Other crab boats were continuing to fish in the area but were still out of sight even from the height of the wave crests.

At that time, we had been out for a week without more than catnaps. By now, we were acting like zombies, and we looked like the living dead, with beards and clothes stained with fish blood and guts, doing what was necessary, taking the risks, in order to fill our holds. We smelled and we ached, and we thought about one thing: money, lots and lots of money.

I was waiting for a weather report from the National Weather Service that would decide for me whether to make a run for shelter in the Pribilofs until the storm blew through. I feel comfortable near the islands as a safe haven, which also provides anchorage for the cannery processing boat that was scheduled to take our catch so that we would not waste precious fuel and time returning to Dutch. We were taking the waves bow-on, when the single sideband over my head in the wheelhouse crackled to life with piercing static. A voice screamed through the speaker, "Mayday! Taking on water. Mayday! This is F/V *Troika*. . . ."

My knees started to shake with anxiety. I glanced at the GPS; the *Troika* was near us, but out of sight. In these seas "taking on water" meant someone on that boat was going to die if we did not reach them in time. We were about twenty-five minutes out. I pulled the switch on the emergency horn, which blared through every nook and cranny on the boat, and I yelled down the stairs into the companionway, "We got a Mayday."

My crew knew what to do without being told. We trained for this. One of us climbed into a survival suit, and the rest of us ran to our stations. Neal headed for the crane controls near the forepeak; the crewman in his survival suit ran for the pot launcher near the crane hook and prepared to throw life rings into the water. Lookouts watched from the stern on both sides. I monitored the radio and took charge of managing the rescue. I did not notify the Coast Guard. By the time they would arrive on the scene the crew and captain of the F/V *Troika* might be dead.

Ten boats converged on *Troika* and were visible as small dots on the plotter. I did not know the *Troika*'s captain, but I knew his boat. She was a crabber, an eighty-foot keelboat from Sand Point. The captain, I recalled from what I had heard, weighed 350 pounds, and stood 6' tall. I learned later that *Troika* was taking on water in the rear lazarette. The stern was swamped. The engine room was flooding. When we finally were close enough to see her through binoculars, the boat listed at a sickening angle to port and was settling lower in the waves with every minute that passed. I threw the throttles against the firewall. *Time Bandit*'s two main diesels roared. In the Bering Sea, time is everything. That day, it was life.

The killer is the sea. The water temperature was around 36 degrees Fahrenheit. Alaska Fish & Game issues a warning about Alaskan waters, describing what happens to a man who falls overboard.

The initial cold shock from falling into cold water provokes an immediate gasp reflex, up to 2–3 quarts of air—or water, if your head is submerged. If you inhale water, it is highly unlikely you will come to the surface unless you are wearing a lifejacket. This means you have to have your lifejacket on when you enter the water! The cold shock stage is characterized by hyperventilation and rapid heart rate, which often produce a panic feeling. This stage lasts 3–5 minutes. The initial shock can also provoke a heart attack, which will make self-rescue extremely difficult. During this period, concentrate on staying afloat and keeping your head above water while you adjust to the shock so you can act more effectively.

I have seen it happen, and Alaska Fish & Game has it partly right. The stages come quickly without a survival suit. The official description fails to describe the differences in human will. Some men give up; others hold on. Some men either rely on their training or lose their judgment completely. In that kind of water, what you think and how you control your emotions can mean the difference between life and death. In the Bering Sea, you have to want to live more than the sea wants you to die, and strange as it seems not everybody wants to live with the same intensity.

I had trained my binoculars on the *Troika*. By now, she was taking waves through the wheelhouse windows and door. I was standing off because the F/V *Marchovi*, another crabber in the fleet, beat us to the rescue. The waves pummeled the stricken boat, which was riding low in the sea. Its failing buoyancy succumbed to the pounding waves. Although the captain could not have known, his boat was done for. The best he could have done was to abandon ship and pray for rescue.

About then, four deckhands jumped into the sea in survival suits. I watched them bob on the waves. I breathed a little easier because I could see they were acting smart. They conserved energy and whatever warmth was left in their bodies, and they used the suits' tethers to stay in a group. I turned my binos from the crewmen to the *Troika*.

She was taking on more water than her pumps could handle. The boat was as good as down. The captain was not going to find the hole where the water was coming in. Repair was out of the question. Time was running out. I watched him cut loose the life raft from the afterdeck. The raft popped open and deployed. I was relieved that he was finally acting to save himself.

At that moment I had my own worries. The sea was rolling my boat. I could not head into the sea and still position myself to assist the *Troika*. Inside the wheelhouse, I was being thrown left and right in a violent motion. I glanced to where I had last seen the gull on the crane boom. It was gone.

Another look through the binoculars told me that the captain of the *Troika* had found a survival suit, but he was not putting it on! I could see its bright red color, and I even started cheering him on. He did not get into the suit. He did not follow his crew into the sea. He disappeared into the engine room, probably diving into the murky water trying to plug up the hole. By now, half the boat was underwater. If he did not help himself soon, the captain was going to be trapped in the cabin. The next I saw of him, he was running through the galley into the wheelhouse. He came out the door with his survival suit still in his arms. Events were overtaking him, and he was not thinking clearly. He was acting like someone who thought the boat still had a chance.

A rogue wave barreled toward him and its force just overwhelmed him. The survival suit flew out of his arms into a gust of wind and disappeared in the spindrift. He was in serious danger now. Too much was happening too quickly, and the consequence of the unfolding events seemed inevitable. I had to try to help him.

The F/V *Marchovi* was the first boat to reach the crew in the water. By the time we had arrived, the *Marchovi*'s captain had positioned his boat with the men in the water along its port side. This approach was wrong. I did not understand why he would be doing this. The *Marchovi*, like us, was rolling hard in the trough. The crane boom was going up and down fifteen or twenty feet with each wave. A wave wall, made of steel and rising to a height of twelve or fifteen feet, higher than a man standing on deck, stretches along the port side at the rail and is designed to protect the crews working on the starboard deck from waves crashing over the boat's port side. Now, with *Marchovi*'s port side to the men in the water, the crane operator and the deckhands ready with the life rings could not see the men in the water.

A crewman threw the life rings over the wall. Another *Marchovi* crewman, dressed in a survival suit, jumped into the water to assist any crewman too weak to grasp the survival rings. While in the water, the crewman attached the picking hook on the crane to a metal ring sewn into the life ring. The hydraulic's operator worked his controls, and in two or three seconds, the picking hook plucked each crewman out of the water and deposited him onto the deck. Another crewman was ready to grab each survivor under his arms and drag him across the deck through the door into the warmth of the cabin, where he undressed, dried himself, dressed in dry clothes, and slipped into a sleeping bag until he began to shiver, which was a first sign that he was no longer hypothermic and would live. The rescue of the crewmen did not take more than a couple of minutes. The survival suits—and the *Marchovi*'s brave crew—had saved four men from dying.

Aboard *Troika*, the captain finally had given up on saving his boat and was fighting to save himself. He grabbed a buoy that was hanging off the side of the boat. He tried to tie a rope around his waist, but before he set a knot, another wave wrenched the buoy from his hands. Now, he was standing *on* the wheelhouse. The boat was straight up and down with the bow out of the water. He climbed on the gunwale but the bow slid farther under. He stepped over to the anchor winch. The boat sank right out from under him.

Now, there *was* no boat. He had nothing left to float on, or in. He was a man in frozen water without a lifejacket or a survival suit. The seas were huge, and the wind was blowing the crests of waves into sheets of stinging spray. The sea and the sky were dark. My anxiety grew with each moment he was out there alone. I was watching from 150 yards away tormenting myself with the thought that I should just barge in to the rescue. It's my personality, my style, to go where I'm not invited. But what if my actions only made the situation worse? I was standing by, useless, when a man's life might depend on me. I saw no good choice.

The *Marchovi* deck crew threw the captain a rope, which he managed to tie around his waist. But the boat rolled at that moment and ripped the rope down his waist and pulled him out of the water by his leg. The picking hook on the crane was snapping up and down with each roll. The rope ripped the captain's boot off. He flew in the air like one of those sea lions being attacked by a killer whale. He just flipped, a big man like that. I thought, *What the fuck!* I'd never seen anything like it. The *Marchovi* took another roll. The *Troika*'s captain tried in vain to grab the tire on the boom. He was desperate and grasping for anything at all to hang on. The boat rolled. He shot up in the air and fell back. That was when he breathed in water.

I yelled out, "Heave ho, I'm coming in."

I could not do worse than the *Marchovi*. I brought up *Time Bandit*'s starboard side to the captain. I knew I could snatch him in a matter of seconds. The crew was waiting. Neal jumped over the side with a survival suit on. We had the sling, the suit, and the picking boom. Neal grabbed the captain and held on. He hooked him on the picking hook, and Andy pulled the two men from the sea. The rescue happened in less than thirty seconds.

The captain was in a bad way. He was hypothermic. It was that single breath of water that was killing him. His core temperature had plummeted. We dragged him into the warmth of the cabin and laid him on the floor of the stateroom nearest the deck door. We laid him on his back on the carpet in the stateroom to the left of the deck hatch. I did not see how he could survive. He had been submerged in the water on the *Troika* up to his chest and then in the water through the wheelhouse. He had been diving into the water in his engine room. When he breathed in the water, his core had chilled beyond his body's ability to recover. There was little we could do for him now. He was unconscious, but he breathed twice. I was bending over him, praying that he would live. Neal was giving him CPR. We could not get him to breathe.

He went, "Pfffff," with a soft deflating sound.

We gave him CPR for two and a half hours. I ran down from the wheelhouse every five minutes. I had called the Coast Guard for guidance. They said to keep him warm and monitor his core temperature with a thermometer. "He isn't dead if he is cold and dead," a Coast Guard flight surgeon told me. "He's only dead when he's *warm* and dead." I stopped taking his temperature.

Finally, the crew leaned back on their haunches. Their faces expressed the truth, and we cried.

I could *feel* the man's soul drift past me.

Imagine! He did not know he was going to die that day. Then suddenly, he faced death and had two chances to save himself. If the *Marchovi* had grabbed him on the first try, he would be alive.

But *he* was the one who made the critical choice to save the boat instead of himself. To be fair, maybe he did not think he was in trouble and if we had come up to him right away, we would have saved him. I knew that. I felt guilty for that. I blamed myself.

We brought his body to the Pribilofs. The EMTs who met us at the dock pronounced him dead. The crew and I used the crane to take off his body. We were standing around in the snow, smoking. We did not talk or look into each other's eyes. A nice lady came up to us. She asked who we were. I had not seen her before on St. Paul. She was crying softly. She said, "I know the family of this man. Thank you for what you did. At least they have a body to bury. He has six young boys." I turned away from her to hide my tears.

We stayed off *Time Bandit* that night. It did not seem right to go back, out of misguided respect. I looked at the sky the following morning. Dark and brooding, it suddenly came alive with bright white gulls. I took off my cap as if I were inside a church. In that moment I believed. A sailor had lost his soul to the sea, and a gull had scooped it up and would follow boats like mine until the end of time.

We returned to *Time Bandit* with trepidation. In the stateroom by the deck door we noticed a dried salt stain on the carpet in the outline of the dead man's body. The sight made me quake. Nobody wanted to talk about it. Nobody made a move to wash it away. I could not confront an image that seemed that directly spiritual. I found a brass key in among others in a galley drawer. I locked the door and hung the key on a string around my neck, like the Ancient Mariner's albatross, where it stayed until last year.

Like Tides in My Veins

Andy

People might laugh if they were to see a Bering Sea crab boat co-captain shoveling horseshit in 90-degree heat, but that's me, and at night, too. My shirt is off and I'm sweating like someone put a hose on me. I am wearing shorts, a straw cowboy hat, and cowboy boots. Attracted by the electric light, moths the size of my fist fill the air, which smells so bad of shit an intake of breath catches in my throat. My stallion Rio stands in the corner like a foreman nodding his approval, wanting me to hurry up so he can go to sleep. This life is not a vacation I am taking from the Bering Sea. I am Andy Hillstrand, and this is the other half of my existence that I do not share with crabs or my brother Johnathan.

Usually, I leave these "housekeeping" chores for the afternoons, but after Russell's call, I could not sit in the house a minute longer.

I have reason to be worried even if it turns out that Johnathan is only late getting in. Our friend, the president of our Bering Sea Crab Co-op, Chris Heuker, drowned two weeks ago in Bristol

Bay, and nobody knows for certain what happened. He was fishing alone, like Johnathan is today. Chris also had a small boat, like Johnathan's *Fishing Fever.* He was a lifelong fisherman, smart, and skilled. He could have had a heart attack. He could have been running the boat from the aft fishing station, again the same as Johnathan on *Fishing Fever,* with throttles and a wheel on the transom only inches from the water with nothing to hold on to. A rogue might have thrown Chris off balance.

Maybe he fell overboard and his boat continued on. Alone in the cold water without a survival suit, drowning was inevitable. He had nobody to rescue him; he could not call for help. Johnathan and I felt saddened by the loss of Chris. We felt terrible for his family. He was the father of teenage boys. He was a great guy and a dedicated, professional co-op manager, and because he was also a fisherman since he was a teenager, fishing was in his blood. Whatever caused his death I am willing to bet he died doing what he loved to do.

After I hung up the phone with Russell, I told Sabrina, "It's about Johnathan."

"What now?" she asked in a tired, been-there-before tone.

I told her.

"What can you do?" she asked.

"Worry," I said. "He's my brother."

She has told me, time and again, "Andy, I would never want to be clinging to a cliff beside Johnathan and have you decide which of us to save. I know who it would be. I'm okay with it not being me." She would usually pause here. "This is not a criticism. It is a fact. And you can't deny it."

I don't. I love Sabrina; I love Johnathan. Just because she does not get into the same perilous scrapes as Johnathan doesn't mean I love her less. In her hypothetical situation, I could not say whom I would save. It is not fair to ask. Sabrina wasn't really asking. She knows. She has had to become a realist. I am a fisherman, an optimist who lives on heapings of denial. We inhabit different planets where philosophies are concerned. She is a fisherman's wife and she has saved my life by making me examine mine. She slowly and painfully came around to understand that when a woman marries a fisherman she shares her man with the sea and with a boat, and barring death and childbirth, he is not coming home until the fishing is done. Actually, forget childbirth. One time, Sabrina nearly died from toxic shock syndrome and I could not get home. She did not expect me to. Like in the military, generals do not stop the war when soldiers' wives are delivering their babies. Maybe a woman strikes a bad bargain when she marries someone like me. The divorce rate of fishermen is high because some women do not understand the men they married. They think they can change them and tame them. They will get them to leave the sea. Right there they have started out wrong. Sabrina knew she would never take me off the sea.

I pat Rio's withers and grab a fistful of his mane, then jump onto his bare back. Together we leave the stall for the paddock. I lean over and open the gate and we head in the direction of the pond, shining in the moonlight. The night is summer-still and hot. Frogs croak in the end of the pond that water lilies have overgrown. There is something so stable about this place, this farm life. I have not regretted moving here for a single moment.

After Dad died Sabrina and I made the move. The timing was no coincidence. Sabrina liked my dad, maybe even loved him, but she saw his faults clearly. She did not like how he treated me. When my brothers and I bought the boat from him, she thought we paid him more than another buyer would have paid. People in Homer believed we had our lives handed to us on a silver platter; in truth, we worked harder than anyone else for our dad, who never helped us. He trained us to survive in the water and taught us to work hard, never to complain, and never quit, but he was a slave driver. Over time, Sabrina grew resentful of him and his ways. He scared her with his drinking. She grew to hate the drunken Christmas arguments and him kicking his sons out of the house. Our children were afraid of him. He said he loved me only three times in his life. In spite of this, I could not leave him. I loved him no matter what.

We bought the farm four years ago. Hobby Horse Acres, as we call it, is about as far from an ocean as anyone can be in the continental United States. We have twelve acres and a pond surrounded by woods, stalls for the horses, riding arenas both indoors and out, and trails. I am proud of the indoor arena, which we built this year; we want the horse-riding business to operate come rain or shine, winter and summer. I should explain, we—Sabrina and I—enjoy the work and wouldn't have it any other way, but Hobby Horse Acres is a struggling business that we plan to make a success through hard work and persistence. From my own perspective, the farm keeps me humble and honest and gives me a different view of life from the sea and commercial fishing. Living and working this far away from the dangers of the sea offers me balance. I should thank horseshit for saving my sanity if not my life.

We found horses the way most people find things—by happenstance. If someone had told me twenty years ago that I would be living on a farm in Indiana raising horses and teaching kids how to ride, I would have laughed. But that was before our daughter Cassie turned eight. We were living in Homer at the time; she told us she wanted a horse for her birthday. All eight-year-old girls want a horse. I wished she had wanted a skiff or for me to take her fishing. And like good parents, we bought her a horse that she named Champ.

That first year after Champ was installed, I was fishing all summer and Sabrina was driving Cassie and her horse to 4H meetings and barrel-racing competitions. Two years went by, and I began to take off the summers to give Sabrina a rest and go to the events with Cassie. I was interested for her as a father. But horses failed to seize my interest, until one day I met a natural horseman, a so-called Whisperer, who asked me if I would like to really get to know horses. *Really?* I had no idea what he meant. He showed me what horses are as creatures, and about them being the ultimate flight animal. Once I understood how a horse thinks I could understand his universe; I approached horses differently, as if we were suddenly equals. I respected him and he understood me. I think that some people deal with horses as if they are machines to be put in gear and driven at different speeds and with maneuvers, like they were motorcycles.

The horse as a unique creature began to intrigue me, and the more I learned about them, the more I was drawn into their world. It was quite different from the one I was used to as a crab fisherman. I enjoyed the new space, which expanded exponentially as I learned and observed. I enjoyed my new friends, the horses. They helped me gain a new perspective on just about everything, including the people I loved and those I would deal with as business associates and friends.

Back then, when this was all new to me, after two weeks of groundwork with the Whisperer's techniques, I won a prize barrel racing at a rodeo. In 1998, I won the Alaska reserve state championship, and for two years running I was state champion. I realized that horses are thousand-pound animals that I did not have to fight. Once you ride a horse and everything is working, it is a beautiful experience and as close to flying, on the ground, as you will ever get. Horses became important in my life. I stopped competitive barrel racing when I reached the understanding that the competition was all about me and not about the horse. The more I learned about them, the more I needed this knowledge. I was learning to be a better person through horsemanship. If I can read body language in a horse without talking to it—by the set of his jaw, his ears, how his eyes blink, where his tail is at—I can look at people's faces and know what they are signaling with their eyes and mouth. I realized that I could help other horse owners with their horses. Now, I look forward to teaching about horses with the same enthusiasm that I once looked forward to fishing.

And yet . . . and yet—isn't there always an "and yet"? In spite of my contentment here, I look forward to Alaska; fishing will never leave my blood, just as it will always be a central part of me. As much as I love the horses and this farm, I feel fully liberated and even wild only when I am on the boat at sea. Nothing will change that. Like tides in my veins, the tug of the land competes with the draw of the sea, and I exist somewhere between.

As much as I love them, horses do not pay for groceries; crabs do.

The aesthetic of fishing never reached me at the same depth as it did Johnathan, who has moments when he even demonstrates a poet's soul when he talks about fish and fishing. He appreciates the beauty of simple things, like the glory of a sockeye's coloring. My daughter Chelsey, who is twenty-six years old, educated and smart, and a new mother of a boy, my grandson Dylan, inherited some of this sensibility.

The spirit of the sea touched her directly a few years ago. At the time—she was just twenty-one, on the night before her grandfather's death. She swears that the *Time Bandit*—yes, the boat my father designed and loved—knew he was going to leave this life. She had taken over the watch on the *Time Bandit*, which was tendering salmon in Bristol Bay. Our brother David was in command. Alone that night in the wheelhouse, Chelsey was doing all that she could to stay alert. An electronic plotter identified the presence of other boats within a radius of forty-eight miles, and David had told her to wake him if a boat appeared within two miles. Suddenly, a boat did appear on the screen identified as the F/V *Guardian.* On the plotter, Chelsey estimated its distance as three miles. It was pitch black out and the boat was on autopilot. Chelsey was daydreaming of an upcoming trip to Europe.

In reality the *Guardian* was less than two miles away and closing fast.

Chelsey squinted in binoculars through the dark, when distances are most deceiving. Through the glare of the sodium lights on the deck she thought the *Guardian* looked still closer but she was not sure. She did not know how to read the navigational screen. "It just didn't seem right," she told me later. "But it didn't seem like an emergency, either."

She went downstairs to wake up a crewman named Chance, who had just gone to bed. She asked him to take a look. Chance saw the *Guardian* was right in front of *Time Bandit.* Chelsey pulled back on the throttles. She slipped the engines in neutral, instead of reverse. And *Time Bandit* moved forward with inertia bringing the two boats together "like two magnets in the sea." Chance threw the *Time Bandit* in reverse too late. The boats collided, "like the Titanic in a small way." Chelsey was looking at the *Guardian* through binoculars even as the two boats screeched in contact. *Time Bandit*'s bow was crushed to the tune of $60,000 in damage. Chelsey prayed to be taken away from her guilt. Eight hours went by in agonizing radio silence before I called her on SatPhone. I was crying; this was the only time she had heard me cry. She supposed it was about the boat accident. Then I told her that her grandfather was dead. Of course, until that moment, she had no idea that timing was an amazing coincidence.

The next morning, Chelsey climbed onto the platform behind *Time Bandit*'s wheelhouse and sobbed. She felt to blame. She had let down the man whose heart was in *Time Bandit* more than anyone's. Suddenly out of that gloom, whales swam in a line on the surface beside the boat and snorted through their blowholes. The whales, she believed, were signaling to her that it was OK. She said to the wind, "Grandpa, thank you, thank you." It was the most profound experience of her young life.

After that, she talked to me about her feelings for the sea. She surprised me when she said, "When I am out there and vulnerable, I am more spiritual than I ever am. The ocean is so powerful and real. If Mother Nature gets mad, I am at her mercy." And what about crabbers like me, her father? "Fishermen live with the notion they can be erased at any moment; they are forced into a camaraderie of survival. On a boat, they know that they have to work together to survive. Alone, they will die. Crabbing is the extreme version of fishing. Crab fishermen are dashing just for what they do. They know that they lay their lives on the line every time they get on a boat, but they can be reassured that their crew will rush to their rescue. This forms a brotherhood. Other men respect them for what they will do. They defer to them in some instinctual way. They envy this brotherhood for its exclusivity. It is very primal, this overcoming of obstacles again and again. It runs in a fisherman's blood. He lives and breathes to do that. More than anything, it is a way of life."

I wish I had that ability to put in those words what I do.

When she told me that, Chelsey was telling me how she had framed a concept of what I do. She asked if I thought that crab fishing has dignity? I did not know what to tell her. I know it is dirty, dangerous, hard work, if that is what she meant by dignity.

She read me an article she had found on the Internet starting with a quote, odd though it seemed to me, from the father of Communism, Karl Marx, who once observed that "Milton produced *Paradise Lost* for the same reason that a silk worm produces silk. It was an activity of his nature." Fishing for crab is not the same as writing an epic poem, but I would agree with the sentiment of that quote. Plying the sea is an essential activity of my nature, as it is of Johnathan's. The article went on. Certain jobs, like crabbing, come with their own "masculine mythology and way of being in the world." Jobs that involve numbers on spreadsheets, for instance, do not come with a code of dignity. Chelsey might be right about that. Nobody at my office, which is *Time Bandit*, ever asks, "I wonder what kind of work I'll be given today? Yeeeaaaaa! A spreadsheet?"

Chelsey finished with this quote: "People in other classes may define the social structure by educational attainment, income levels and job prestige, but," Chelsey said, men like me and Johnathan "are more likely to understand the social hierarchy on the basis of who can look out for themselves, who has the courage to be a fireman, a soldier or a cop, who has the discipline to put bread on the table every night despite difficulties." Everyone else is a manipulator.

The way I see my work is not that complicated; it's what I love. Other men have golf, hunting, fishing, and other outlets to nourish their spirits. A man can do the shittiest job during the week if he can look forward to his softball team or golf on Saturdays. That is how most guys survive. When they meet someone like Johnathan and me, no matter what walk of life they come from, something in them responds. It's like they are saying, "My God, you are doing something I'd die to do."

I feel good about working. I can fix things. It is as simple as that. And I can outwit, most of the time, the humble crab or the predictable salmon. I fix stuff all the time; I get it running good again. I am doing that all the time. People need me. I am needed for doing things, not just thinking things. I put the two things together to produce something that works. I know how to use my hands, and anyone who has ever worked with his hands knows me, knows what I do, and who I am. Out on *Time Bandit*, I am fixing stuff all the time. It is satisfying in ways other work just is not. Fixing things gives me a sense of my own worth that I can measure in simple terms. I fix what I try to fix. Like if I have to fix my wife I say, "You look good, honey. Those pants look great on you."

"They make me look fat, don't they?"

"Oh, no, honey." See? I just fixed something.

On *Time Bandit* I do not have bosses telling me what to do. Nobody is nagging me. Guys get that.

When I meet contractors and builders, plumbers and electricians and deliverymen who fish for bass when they can, I realize how much bullshit they put up with each day—that traffic on the commute to and from work, demanding bosses, and little offices. Why do they not make a run for it? They have responsibilities, families, obligations, the love of their wives and children. And they keep quiet about the bullshit in return for two weeks of fishing each year, or whatever nourishes their souls. Fifty weeks pays for two. To these men, I am free; they are chained. When Johnathan and I finish a season, we go where the wind blows us. And when I am out fishing, I am like the cowboy who rides off into the sunset at the end of the movie, leaving the woman and kids, the ranch, the whole life behind. That was why our old man loved to read Louis l'Amour. The cowboy goes away. . . . alone or with a posse in a brotherhood of men. And that is what men are made to do. Women may not like to hear it. I am certain of that. But they acknowledge this primitive urge as a fundamental need that nothing will change.

Some of that explains why the impulse to worry for Johnathan seems so natural and right for me. It's part of The Code.

It's time to go in. I cluck my tongue and Rio nickers. He knows where I want him to go. I pat him on the neck. And as I do so, Johnathan comes back to mind. He will have me worrying the whole night. It is part of a pattern, as Sabrina says. It is hardly a revelation that family roles do not change with age. Mamma's boy will always be. I cover for Johnathan, and always have. I have been there for him as long as he has been alive. Usually, I drag him out of the fights before they get mean, and I have finished some fights for him. I have watched out for him because that is my role. It is not his role to watch out for me. In fact, his role in the family is never to grow old. I have no one to protect if I do not have Peter Pan. And we both understand that. I once heard about two brothers in their mid-fifties who were fighting at their mother's 80th birthday party. Why? Because one thought that their mother loved the other brother more. Well, it is what it is, and nothing is going to change it.

It is not the mother thing between us. We are not worried that she loves us. Indeed, she might love us too much. She constantly reminds us of the dangers of what we do for a living, as if we did not know that after a lifetime of fishing for crabs. She prays for us when we are out on the Bering Sea. She asks us to please find safer work on land. Lately, she announced that she had given up that hope. She would no longer worry about us. Johnathan looked at me. He said, "That's bad news."

What set our roles was our age difference of only one year. We grew up together. John was small until he was a late teenager and I watched out for him. The teenage world can be a nasty place and he was a combination of vulnerable and invulnerable. He has a tough and a soft side. I have to keep watch on his soft side. I do not want to see that part of him destroyed. Indeed, I do not want to see any part of him destroyed. And that desire has put me now in a state of worry that will not end until I hear his voice.

In the stall again, I tell Rio good night, and I head through a gate across a lawn and through a garden, which Sabrina tends with devotion. The night scent of *Mirabilis jalapa*, Sabrina calls the golden flower, welcomes me along the path to the door. For the next couple of hours, I sit and stare at the telephone.

We Started Throwing Fists

Johnathan

I am *not* lost at sea. I do not know where I am, but I just do not feel lost—*yet* anyhow. I curl up on the bunk in the wheelhouse. It is getting dark. The wind is blowing up. The sea is getting sloppy. I fire up a Winston and stare out the port windows. And I see nothing but an endless plane of water without a seam between sea and sky. I could be a farmer in the midst of a vast field of grain. I *am* a farmer, tilling the sea on a busted tractor.

In Anchorage two days ago, I was talking about crabs. Fish in general can be a man's excuse for talking, a conversational port that leads to oceans of possible humor, exaggeration, storytelling, personal insights, and folk truths. It is socially safe—in the sense of being noncommittal. And it helps a stranger to get to know someone else without grilling him. For a lot of men, conversing about fish with a commercial fisherman like myself is like a weekend softball player sitting down with Barry Bonds: informative, suspenseful, and floated on a wave of bullshit. I see even awe in some men I meet in bars. They will start a conversation about fishing to hear what fishing is like in the big leagues, and I do not kid myself. I know that to them crab fishing on the Bering Sea is like the outer edge of extreme sports, like climbing El Capitan without safety ropes or surfing a 100-foot wave off Palau. When strangers ask me to talk about crabbing on the Bering, I oblige. After fishing and women and my children, bullshit is the love of my life. I have told a few tales many times. Sometimes I hear myself telling them in my sleep. Not that repetition bothers me. With women, commercial crab fishing talk presents a view into a man's world in which they can sit back and watch the fun. In Anchorage, an attractive woman at the table who had nothing to do with the sea, whom I had never met before, asked me how I was able to tell a male from a female crab, one being legal and the other being illegal to catch. The question was certainly valid, I thought, but I did not feel like giving her a serious answer. I told her, "You can tell the male crab from the female crab because the male crab is usually on top." She looked at me cautiously not knowing how to react. Then she smiled, I thought seductively.

Her ignorance, while understandable, illustrated a more interesting point—that we live today far removed from the origins, even from a passing knowledge, of what we eat from the land or the sea. Fishermen, like farmers, see the food up close from its origin to its delivery to market. We crabbers know from the ocean floor up that a crab is a weird being. Its ugly design brings to mind Jonathan Swift's famous quip. "'Twas a brave man who first et an oyster." Indeed, who first discovered that there was anything under a crab's carapace to eat at all?

True crabs have ten legs in five pairs, and look like spiders. The first pair of legs bears their claws or pincers, and the right claw, called the "crusher," is usually the largest on the adults. The next three pairs are their walking legs, and the fifth pair is small and normally tucked underneath the rear portion of their shell. Adult females use these specialized legs to clean their fertilized eggs; males use them to transfer sperm to the female during mating.

Crabs live at depths of 400-feet plus in darkness and in water the temperature of liquid ice. They feed off rich nutrients that well up from the Aleutian Basin. They sense the presence of our bait through chemoreceptors; the crab has a hardiness that its shell alone does not do justice to. Their ballast system is amazing. Their blood is white, made of hemocyanin, and flows with powerful quick-acting coagulants that allow them to recover instantaneously from even the most grievous injuries and amputations. Their spiny shells protect them from natural predators like cod, and their beady black eyes, standing on short stalks just ahead of their brains, cover a field of vision adequate to detect enemies in time to react with their pincers.

Crab legs, besides being delicious steamed in seawater and served with a brush of butter, fascinate crabbers. Last year in king crab season, the crew on a break was talking about king crabs' pincers, particularly "the crusher," which has the power to snap ballpoint pens in half. In something less than a scientific observation, Andy informed us that "Guys have had their dicks grabbed by the crusher."

Russell's eyes brightened. "Is that a common method of catching a crab, Andy?"

Opilio and king crabs can be easily sexed—to answer the woman in Anchorage in a more serious vein. The male abdomen, which curves under the crab's throat, is narrow in males; in females it is considerably wider to assist in carrying the fertilized eggs. King crabs have "tails" or abdomens that are distinctively fan-shaped and tucked underneath the rear of their shell.

Adult females produce thousands of embryos. When these

fully develop they become swimming larvae and drift with the tides and currents. They feed on plant and animal plankton while their bodies undergo rapid changes. Red king crab larvae later settle to the bottom of particularly cold waters. In order to grow, they need to rehouse themselves in new shells every so often. Adult male king crabs keep one shell for as many as two years before molting and growing a new one. Red Alaskan king crabs, the largest of the crab species with the record female weighing twenty-four pounds and an average male weighing around ten and a half pounds, live for twenty to thirty years. The male's leg can reach a span of six feet. We catch them all the time with spans of four feet plus.

The adult crabs, like many other species, live in groups divided by sex when they are not molting or mating. The males can migrate up to 100 miles in a year, moving at times as fast as a mile per day in massed male-only configurations, like rolling balls on the sea floor. They eat worms, clams, mussels, snails, brittle stars, sea stars, sea urchins, sand dollars, barnacles, other crustaceans, fish parts, humans if they can find one, sponges, algae—and *other* king crabs. And they are eaten by cod, halibut, octopuses, sea otters, nemertean worms—and *other* king crabs.

Alaskan natives have eaten these sea spiders since before recorded time, but who would have guessed that crabs would take off as an international delicacy? The commercial crab industry in Alaska started in 1950 when hundreds of U.S. fishermen entered a race every bit as frenzied as a gold rush. By the 1980s Alaska king crab boat captains regularly were earning well in excess of $150,000 in a season. The money was unprecedented, and crabbing was viewed as an endless road paved with gold. But in 1983, the industry simply collapsed. No one knows why.

Whether the water temperature changed or a virus infected the crabs or whether overfishing tipped the species' ability to regenerate itself, the crabs disappeared. We thought we had the crabs beat, too, with our large boats, big tanks, cranes and launchers, plotters and scanners. But we were wrong. In the end, the crabs reminded us of a simple lesson. While crabbing might call itself an industry, it is still fishing, and fishing is a part of nature, which man cannot tame, box, predict, or prod. It refuses to be controlled and is what it is and always will be. We live by its rules, not ours. We like to think that we are in control. As seafarers we *must* think that. Otherwise, we would not be able to summon the courage to face the storms. In our hearts we know that we have nothing to say about crabs, whether they will be there to catch or disappear. We have nothing to say about the crabs' environment, the sea, except that either we will venture forth to fish or we won't. I imagine this sounds simplistic to some people. I might agree with them. But I wonder about these issues.

I was one of those fishermen who went east in response to the collapse of the Bering Sea crab fishery, which was recorded as the worst slump in U.S. fishing history. I was reading in a fisherman's journal that New Bedford, Massachusetts, was the number one fishing port in the United States. I flew straight there. I bought the F/V *Hannah Boden*, the sister ship of the F/V *Andrea Gail*, of *Perfect Storm* fame. The contract was written on a napkin. We grossed $800,000 in four months. I worked my ass off. The owner refused to honor the napkin contract, and I bought F/V *Canyon Explorer*, an eighty-eight-foot lobster boat that we fished eighty miles off Cape Cod. We fished around the clock. For the most part, the local crews I hired were worthless. They liked to sleep. They stayed at the dock, and I had to hire replacements from the homeless shelter; I would take any able-bodied man I could find. Even with a wooden boat and with no cranes I still kicked ass.

I thought of the East Coast fishermen; compared to us from Alaska, they can sometimes be stubborn, like the Maine lobstermen with five or six generations of fishermen behind them. Many of them, to this day, are good friends who sometimes tend to think of the Atlantic as *their* ocean. They did not like me fishing George's Bank. I asked them, "Are you George?" A lot of them did not like me. It's hard not to like me. They came around eventually. They are a proud breed, some of them, anyway . . .

The worst fight I ever got in was in Providence, Rhode Island, on Christmas Eve. Two friends from Alaska and I were sitting at a nice, respectable piano bar, and one of them said he knew of a good club. I thought, no. I'll just stay here, have a few drinks, and then go back to the hotel and go to bed. I ended up bleeding half to death a couple hours later. We went to a place called Club Hell. We checked our coats. One guy was wearing a $500 leather jacket that he was particularly pleased with. We were given coat checks.

We had a nice time, dancing and joking and drinking, but when we were leaving, the employee who had checked our coats said he never gave us tags. He did not have our coats. They were gone. We showed him the tags and he said sorry. That was how the fight started. I said that we were not leaving without our fucking coats. The bouncers appeared. "Yes, you are leaving," is what one of them said. We started throwing fists. This big fucker waded in. He was like Jaws in the James Bond movie, a freak of nature. He was the biggest sonofabitch I ever saw in my life. I drew him. I was about to learn why they called it Club Hell.

Jaws picked me up by my crotch and by my neck, ran with me, and threw me against a Porsche parked out in front. I'm a 205-pound guy, but to him I was like a little bitch. There was nothing I could do. An alarm in the Porsche went off. The bouncer's friends were kicking me. Jaws picked me up again and threw me into a brick wall. I was saying to myself, "Why did I go to Club Hell?" One of my buddies, Clark Sparks, who drowned a month later, tried to help me, but a bouncer knocked him out. I thought, "I'm going to die in Providence, Rhode Island, on Christmas Eve." When the cops showed up, I hugged them. They gave me a ride to my hotel. I was bleeding in my hips and bled through the mattress. I got over it, but from that moment I made my plans to return to the serenity of Alaska.

Last year, once we returned from Latitudes, we had plenty of work still left to do before the king crab season started. We loaded up our freezers in the forepeak with boxes of pinks and chum salmon for king crab bait. For opilios later in the season, we rely on cod and chopped herring for bait. But for king crab, we snap in two salmon per pot, and in opilio season we will load four cod per pot. The king season is open for thirty days but we plan to catch our quota in seven. We estimated that we would pull 120 pots a day, or 840 pots total. That meant we needed ten pounds of salmon for each pot, or 8,400 pounds of bait. We try to use all the bait in one season. Otherwise, we need to either throw it out the scuppers at a loss or save it in the freezers for next season.

We still had the Coast Guard to contend with, and our own issues of safety. We see enough of the Coasties at the bars in Dutch to know them, and we consider them allies and, some of them, friends. We respect who they are and what they do. Our lives may depend on them.

Last year, in a bar in Kodiak town, I ran into Matthew Thiessen, a rescue swimmer for the Coast Guard, based at Air Station Kodiak. For recreation, Matt *surfs* in freezing Alaskan waters, to give you an idea of his toughness. He hit the water last year to rescue four crewmen on the F/V *Hunter*, a fishing boat that sank in the Shelikof Strait in winter. His story is only one of probably hundreds the Coast Guard could tell about rescuing fishermen on the Bering Sea, but the *Hunter* tale illustrates for me what these guys go through for our safety.

Matt never saw the boat. *Hunter* sank quickly. An EPIRB in the water alerted the Coast Guard's Alaska headquarters in Juneau, which diverted a CG C-130 Hercules already in flight to take a look around for survivors from about 2,000 feet. They spied a life raft in the water, and Matt and his helicopter crew were called out. From their ready room in Kodiak they ran across a concrete apron to an H-60 Jayhawk military helicopter parked in a hangar. Matt sat in the back of the chopper, running the radios. He was wearing a dry suit with fleece long johns, boots, and a flight helmet. When the helo reached the raft and hovered, ice warning lights lit up in the Jayhawk's cockpit. Ice was forming on the rotor blades in temperatures of 10 degrees below zero. The *Hunter*'s crew had been in the raft for more than an hour. Matt took off his flight helmet and put on his flippers and neoprene headgear for warmth. He snapped the hoist cable to a rock-climbing harness he wears, and with a Triton harness carrying his gear, like flares and a radio and such, he headed down. The shock of cold water hit him. The raft was clipping away from him at around four knots in the wind. He swam like hell and got a hand on it. Four crewmen looked at him from under the raft's awning. They were wearing survival suits, but he said that just by looking at their faces, he knew that two of them were in bad shape. They were in shock, and water had leaked into their survival suits. The *Hunter*'s captain had stripped down his suit until he was naked to his waist, in serious shock and in denial; hypothermia can make men believe that they are hot, and this illusion can kill them.

Matt grabbed the first crewman and took him into tow. A man-sized metal basket was lowered from the helicopter. Matt worked to get him into the basket in seas that continually flipped the man out. He was not helping his own cause. He was rigid and his right arm was stiff, and Matt had to bend him to get him into the basket. The first crewman was finally hoisted up. By the time Matt turned around to reach for the next crewman, the wind had blown the raft away, and without explanation, the helicopter left—just disappeared. Matt treaded water alone for the next fifteen minutes, wondering what was going on. He told me he thought in back of his head, "I got three more guys to rescue and I'm pretty winded. I have no helicopter and I don't know what to do."

The Jayhawk finally did return and hovered. Matt used a strop to hoist the second man, then rode the cable up to the Jayhawk to warm up. That helped. And he went back down into the sea for the last two. The third crewman was hard to reach. The raft continued to move with the wind. The Jayhawk hoist operator and cockpit crew had put Matt down broadside to the raft. He had to sprint for two minutes in the water to reach the raft only a few feet away. It would have stayed beyond his reach if a swell had not surfed him to it. Water had leaked into the captain's survival suit. He was heavy to start with. Matt was afraid that the additional weight of the water in the survival suit would tug the captain out of the sling. He told him to relax and let the hoist operator do the work. Matt said the man had a look in his eyes that said, "I'm not going to make it." The hoist line took the load. He was winched to safety. The last survivor, by comparison, was easier.

The four rescued men off the *Hunter* were hypothermic, two seriously so. They were out of the water and in danger of drowning but not yet out of danger. It was Matt who told me the horror of serious triage performed in huge waves of icy 36-degree water. If he is faced with several bodies in the water, and his resources to save all of them are few, he has to make hard choices. He said the specter of this happening keeps him awake at night. In only seconds he must evaluate and prioritize consciousness, breathing, and circulation. He has to ask himself who is the most salvageable. I could never do that, and neither could most people I know. It would be playing God.

Matt has dealt with some hard cases. One time he was lowered to the deck of a boat to rescue a fisherman whose body was caught on a steel winch drum. The initial report indicated that the man was already dead. Matt was going to pick up the body. But when his feet touched the boat's deck, the man looked at him with knowing eyes. He was still alert and trying to tell him something but noise of the helicopter drowned out his words. The man gave him a look that said, "I'm not done yet." He was lashed to the drum by tight strands of two-inch braided nylon rope, which was connected to a supply boat they had been towing. The rope had broken both the man's lower legs and femur bones and his pelvis, and part of his scalp was peeled off. Miraculously, he survived.

The same thing nearly happened to Andy one time when he and I were out alone on my boat, *Arctic Nomad*, long-lining for halibut in the Cachemak Inlet near Homer. A current was running about five knots, and the line, as a result, kept popping out of the gerdie, a hydraulically driven drum on which the long lines wrap themselves as they are brought in, hopefully heavy with hooked halibut. The line had wrapped around Andy. I quickly pulled the boat out of gear. The line was squeezing him and would have cut him in half or pulled him overboard and drowned him. Or he would have lost both arms. Andy was screaming, "Cut the line, cut the line!" I whipped my knife out of the scabbard and ran to the back deck from the wheelhouse. I was not thinking where to cut the line. I was close to panic. If I had cut the line behind my brother he might not have come out alive. We laughed so hard with relief we were crying.

Like anyone who works on the sea, Matt is constantly surprised by human endurance and the will to survive. He deals all the time with people on the edge in extreme circumstances. Some people just give up, but mostly, he said, they fight. One man he went to rescue on the Bering Sea had caught his arm in a winch. The bone was broken, the muscles were strung out, and the pain was excruciating. The man was eerily calm, sitting on the deck holding his arm and smoking a cigarette, waiting for the helicopter to arrive. At the same time, others who are barely in any danger freak out. He reflected on serendipity, the chance of the sea. He shook his head.

I thought about the F/V *St. Patrick*, December 2, 1981. She was a 158-foot scallop boat with a crew of eleven that ran into a storm at night five miles west of Marmot Island, near Kodiak. She took on water in her engine compartment and listed 90 degrees, balanced on the edge of going over. The crew put on survival suits, tied themselves together, and abandoned ship; the life raft was lost. The crew, fearing that the boat would turn over on them, swam as far away as they could before exhaustion overcame them. The current and the winds did the rest. Eight crewmen and one woman drowned or died of hypothermia that day and the next. Two survived. The agony of the *St. Patrick* was that she had righted herself after the crew had abandoned ship; a Coast Guard cutter towed her into port. They would all be alive if only they had stayed with her.

The same was true twenty years ago of a scow that was sinking off Kodiak in a bad storm. The crew of six had five survival suits. The cook lost out. The crewmen jumped overboard, and the cook opened a bottle of liquor and got drunk at the galley table. He passed out, and when he woke up the storm had gone past, and he was alive. The crewmen who had jumped over-board died of hypothermia.

Another of Matt's surprises, he told me, is the size and invis-ibility of a man in the sea. He said a human head in the water is no larger than a floating basketball. "You can miss people," he told me, with the search helicopter flying at 200 feet and 80 knots. "You can miss them so easily it makes you want to cry."

That is the best part of the Coast Guard. The worst is their watchdog powers over *Time Bandit*, its safety gear, and our train-ing to react in a crisis. I tend to think the Coast Guard has it out for me for what I did once on a day that was blowing 50 in the harbor, and *Time Bandit* lost steering as we were coming in. I called the Coast Guard to tell them I had no steering, and I put bumpers and buoys over the side. But we slammed the Coast Guard's big cutter *Roanoke Island* anyway. The officers in charge could not see this merely as an accident. They thought I was drunk and gave *Time Bandit*'s crew and me drug tests.

I can usually talk to anyone. And Andy can talk to horses. He reads people like he reads his horses. So I leave the Coast Guard inspections for him to handle. Sometimes, I see a twenty-year-old Coastie come on *Time Bandit* who wants only to rip me a new one. I get out of the way. They come onboard and get up our butts like rubber coconuts. They tell us we cannot leave port until we get this fixed or that fixed or this or that done. We have too many pots on deck. Andy gets out the calculator, and not only do we not have too many, we have too few. The Coastie starts arguing over pot size and weight.

When they boarded us last year, three Coasties asked for our crew's licenses, which they inspected and noted on their clip-boards. They checked *Time Bandit*'s papers. They counted extin-guishers and flares, the Satellite 406 EPRIBs, life rings, life rafts, and the integrity and check-by dates of our survival suits. They

Getting into trouble:
Johnathan (left) and Andy,
four and three years old

Johnathan's (left, age four) and Andy's (age three) first flounders

Try Again, our childhood "pirate boat"

Grandma Jo Shupert,
1945

Ice fishing on the Bering Sea, 2006

Unloading opies at St. Paul, the Pribilof Islands

Old *Bandit*. On deck: Dad (middle), Neal (left), Andy and Johnathan (right)

Andy and crewmate at the pot block getting ready to throw the hook

Andy's girls:
Sabrina, Chelsey,
Cassie

Sabrina running the crane

Johnathan with his king salmon catch, early '80s

Neal in the tank, 1986

Grandma Jo, Johnathan's son, Scott, and Mom

Downtime on the *Time Bandit*: Johnathan (left) and Andy playing video games
(© Sabrina Hillstrand)

Andy in a survival suit

Andy barrel racing (© Sabrina Hillstrand)

Andy (left) and Johnathan in Florida, 2007, with a 10 ft. 2 in. gator

Malcolm doing the survival-suit drill

Sorting opies: Johnathan (left), Richard Gregoire, and Shea Long (far right)

Neal with Bandit

Johnathan's "cooler" Harley

Johnathan with two monster crabs

Johnathan's Harley burning rubber

Fish camp around the oil-drum fire. Russ, Dino, and Johnathan

Taking aim: Johnathan, 2007

Fishing Fever, Johnathan's salmon boat, on the grid

Andy with Cali and Bait

Andy (right) with Dad

Magnetic darts at fish camp set where we would fish

looked carefully at our stability letter, which states how many pots we can safely carry on deck. Intentional or not, miscalculations (inputting the wrong pot weights) have in the past caused ships to capsize and now pot weight is monitored to the pound. The Coasties behaved in a formal, professional manner. Then, before they went away, they detonated a smoke bomb in our engine room and shouted "Fire!"

I hit the switch in the wheelhouse for the warning sirens, and all hands ran to their stations. We followed the smoke belowdecks. I threw on a re-breather and without triggering it, I aimed an extinguisher at the "flame," which I soon "put out." The Coasties stood by, watching us scurry around in utter seriousness. We did not go through the drills exactly as prescribed. We used common sense that often gets left out of the written regulations. The Coasties debriefed us. They wanted to know what we could have done better. And we talked about it. They brought up other scenarios, like a hole in the boat, abandon ship, flooding, a Mayday, the whole drill. We must have passed muster, because they then proceeded to the next tests with survival suits and deployment of our ten-man raft.

Getting into a survival suit is no mean feat even for someone agile, trim, and calm. But panic can scramble brains. The survival suit is the first line of defense on the Bering Sea. The crewmen keep them within an arm's reach when they are sleeping. When the alarms ring and either Andy or I order the crew into their suits, they have sixty seconds to shake out the bag, lay the suit out on the floor, sit down, push their legs in, stand up, push their arms in, pull up the long lariat on the zipper, put the hood over their heads, and close the Velcro flap over their mouths. It is a struggle but beats the alternative.

We waddled to the rail. I had assigned Russell the life raft duties. He jettisoned a hard plastic chamber that was bolted to the

top of the wheelhouse on the aft deck. The raft deployed automatically when it hit the water. As usual, the Coasties asked us
to follow the raft in. That always gives me pause. The water is so
feared by us, even a trial run triggers a feeling of dread. In our
minds, Bering Sea water equals death. We balk even when we
know that the dock is only feet away.

We took our positions on the rail, crossed one forearm over
our faces with our palm over our mouths, and jumped. Once the
water closed around me, even though this was Dutch Harbor, I
imagined myself in a real crisis. The exercise took hold of me
with a seriousness that surprised me. One by one, we swam to
the raft and struggled in on our stomachs until the Coasties told
us to come back onboard *Time Bandit*.

Once the Coast Guard was finished with us, we were not
done. Next, we were visited by the state government in the presence of Fish & Game and the federal government in the guise of
National Marine Fisheries Service, which itself is part of NOAA.
Once, OSHA boarded us with the unwanted news that we were
using the wrong kind of welding gear. Sometimes these agency
representatives can be adversarial, but most of the time they are
trying to help. Andy and I have wondered if the space shuttle has
this much oversight.

In the end, I doubt that crab fishing could be made safer than
what it already is and still remain efficient and cost effective. *Time
Bandit* is eminently stable, as I have said. We carry fewer pots than
we are allowed. We use the latest firefighting equipment. We take
extra precautions with the crew. We train. We treat fishing on the
Bering Sea as the serious, unforgiving task that it is.

Now, two chores remained before we could leave Dutch to
begin our season in the fall of 2006. We wanted to be out on the
king crab grounds in the southeast Bering Sea near the Bristol
Bay line before the season officially opened. For an irrational rea-

son that has to do with our competitive natures, we wanted to be the first to drop pots on the opening hour of crab season, even though with our IFQs, the date hardly mattered. Last season we knew what we would catch. But we worried about making our delivery dates with the processors. If we missed our appointment by only a couple of hours, we would have had to go to the back of the line, risking the loss of the crabs in our holds. Sometimes the wait can be days.

Neal and I led the way from the dock in our rented SUV. He had lists. I had only preferences. Driving over to Dutch's Eagle Quality Center in snow flurries, I noticed an unusual number of bald eagles soaring over the canneries and the hillside that runs down to the harbor. Eagles are as numerous on Dutch as pigeons in a park; they are glorious and beautiful to watch as they swoop over the road. We drove through puddles and ruts in the gravel road that leads away from the canneries toward the commercial section of the harbor. Everything on Dutch wears the cold gray coat of winter, from the sky to the land. This is not a pretty island. Like *Time Bandit*, its purpose is work.

Neal and I each wheeled a shopping cart into Eagle's, which looks like a warehouse with high ceilings of structural braces and conduits for heat and ventilation. The rows of grocery shelves are spaced to allow fishermen to wheel large platform dollies for their groceries. I doubt if anyone comes here for only a quart of milk.

I ran through the aisles scooping groceries into a cart with my arms. Neal, meanwhile, checked his long list. He was hunting for "specials." We needed to buy enough food to feed seven hungry, active men for two weeks. I concentrated on cigarettes and Copenhagen. Candy came next. The candy drawer on *Time Bandit* empties out first at sea; the crewmen call candy "deck steaks" because often when they are working, Snickers and Hershey's bars are the only food they have time to eat. Next to go into the cart were snacks like Cheez Puffs and Doritos. I told Russell to load up a separate cart with drinks like Red Bull, Amp and Full Throttle and half-gallon plastic bottles of Coke and root beer. Neal selected a choice eighteen-pound rib-in roast. I scooped in boxes of Saltines. I passed the magazine racks. In the cart went *Maxim*, the latest *Plumpers*, National Geographic's *Adventure*, *Sailing*, *FHM*, *Vanity Fair*, *PC*, *Rolling Stone*. . . . The next items on my list were less-quick snacks, peanut butter and jelly and bologna and salami, Poppin' Fresh muffins, Hot Pockets. The carts were quickly getting full. Neal bought thirty dozen eggs to cook; I stacked on ten dozen eggs in my cart to throw at the crew. Neal carefully counted twenty big cans of Folgers coffee. I reached for the Tabasco and Reddi-wip. We lined up the carts, and when the checkout woman finished scanning the products, the total came to $5,488.

With the groceries packed in the SUV, we stopped to buy personal gear. Metal racks of slickers and shelves of T-shirts and sweatshirts inscribed with "Eat Crab" and "Eat Fish," bib overalls, Grundens, gloves, knives, hand warmers, and woolen hats lined the shed. Shea bought new Grundens, and I bought an armful of sweatshirts. The personal gear is less an afterthought than a simple staple; we wear the same sweatshirt and T-shirts for days. Personal items such as shaving cream, razors, gel, and deodorants have no place on the Bering Sea and are left back in port. Some fishermen believe the superstition that shaving at sea brings bad luck. We will probably never know, because no one ever shaves on *Time Bandit* while she is out of port. No one in the crew cares what anyone else looks like or if they smell rank with sweat and putrefying fish slime.

Virtually every deckhand dresses in waterproof orange Grundens' Herkules bib pants and hooded parkas, often writing their name in black marker across the backs. Baseball hats turned backward, as a practical matter, are de rigueur. Around our waists we string webbed belts to which we attach scabbards for short, razor-sharp knives; on deck the knife, cutting through a line tangled on a man's leg, has saved lives. We wear thick warm socks in Xtratuf rubber boots and blue-lined gloves to protect our hands from cold and wet. What we wear under our slickers we choose for warmth—hooded sweatshirts over T-shirts or sweat pants or jeans.

Next we made a final stop at the Unisea Sports Bar for a last good-bye.

Sig Hansen was in attendance off the *Northwestern*. He is a great fisherman. I have no higher praise. Larry Hendricks off *Sea Star* was talking; if InSauna bin Russell wanted to torture Larry he would need only to put him in a cell with no one to listen to him. Last year when Larry and I were sharing a hotel room, I ducked into the bathroom to tell him that Andy and I were leaving for dinner. Larry stepped out of the shower and gave me a full frontal. I needed a support group to help me get over the shock. Larry told me that his strategy last year was to "plug the boat," as if everyone else had a strategy of returning empty. Blake Painter off *Maverick* was looking preoccupied; this was his first king crab season as captain. Keith Colburn, captain of *Wizard*, was trading yarns with the bartender, and Phil Harris off the *Cornelia Marie* was talking about his sons, who were going along as green-horns. Phil was telling someone, "You get out and get in fast, if you can, to duck death. You always hope it's not your time." I overheard one of the crewmen talking to Sarah, the Sports Bar's cute, blond, Swedish bartender, about "the lifestyle of danger," and I rolled my eyes at her and she laughed. We sat around a table and swapped stories and bragged. Everyone shared the same feeling of new beginnings, and what was past was past.

Sitting around a table near the bar, while Russell bellowed karaoke—I think it was the Stones's "Satisfaction"—the captains of five boats—*Cornelia Marie, Time Bandit, Northwestern, Maverick,* and *Wizard*—proposed bets on which boat would catch the most king crabs; to make the betting fair, I suggested that the winner would have the highest numbers of crabs per pot, not the highest numbers overall, since the catch varied from boat to boat according to IFQs. We bet $100 each, which the manager of the Unisea Sports Bar kept for us until the season ended.

The bet was not over money, per se. The highest per-pot numbers would go to the captain and crew who were the better fishermen, knew where to find the hot spots for the crabs, calculated the right baits and soaking times, and in the end just got luckier than everyone else. That was what the bet was really about. Sig, who has an ego, thought he already had won. Everyone else would have raised the bet. A gathering of crab boat captains never wants for self-confidence.

We drank and bragged and smoked until we were, most of us, drunk and hoarse. We wandered in groups according to boat crews out into a cold starry night ready at last to face the Bering Sea for a share of the $60 million jackpot of Alaskan king crab.

7

No Such Luck

Once he had cleared the Kasilof estuary Russell discovered that
Rivers End had no single sideband and the VHF channel 16 had a
range of only 20 miles. Russell used his cell phone instead to call
the Coast Guard while he was still in range. When he was
patched through to the Kodiak duty officer and inquired whether
they had heard from *Fishing Fever*, the Coastie told him no, he had
not. Russell asked him to keep a watch on the general area where
he thought Johnathan might be found. The Coastie asked him
why he thought that Johnathan might be missing and Russell told
him that Johnathan was his friend and he *was* missing, or overdue anyway. The bit about being late into harbor did not seem to
move the Coast Guardsman, who recorded the information duti-
fully, Russell was sure, but they both knew that the Coast Guard
could do nothing until daylight, if even then. Normally they did
not leap into action without definitive information that a boat was
lost or capsized and dead in the water, and they had a general fix.
Russell had nothing of that sort to give him. He asked if Russell

knew whether *Fishing Fever* was carrying an EPIRB emergency beacon. Certainly not, he told him, adding to the list a survival suit, a life raft, and maybe not flares or a life jacket. Russell heard him say, "Sorry, sir."

The magnetic darts that the men in camp threw in the direction of the naked lady drawing on the van and how Johnathan's had hit the lower regions gave Russell a general direction to follow. Dino had said, "He went south of the line." That sounded like Johnathan marching to his own drummer. He would have chosen that area, the magnetic dart notwithstanding, because he was the better fisherman among the men in camp. He would have known, for instance, the direction the sockeyes were taking toward their home rivers. He can smell the fish. He gets inside their heads. He knows even before they do what they will do. He might as well *be* half salmon. He would have been trying to find them as soon as they entered the Cook Inlet. That would mean fishing closer to shore and farther south toward the Inlet's wide mouth in waters that become increasingly dangerous the farther south and west a boat goes. He would have tried to separate himself from the other boats no matter what. Johnathan's *Fishing Fever* was fast, easily reaching sustained speed above 20 knots. He would have been away and off radar before anybody noticed.

Russell had a thought. The Alaska Wildlife Troopers, a division of the State Police, had a surveillance system for boats in the salmon fishery, which was the largest in Alaska. Fines for infractions were hefty but to find violators the State Police patrolled immense areas of ocean with only 80 field officers. And therefore, they had brought technology to bear. The State Police patrolled the Cook Inlet salmon grounds in airplanes. From the vantage of height, they viewed the entire fleet and marked any boat that set its gill net as few as two seconds before the 7 a.m. opening. Could spotters in the airplane have seen *Fishing Fever*?

He called them on VHF patched through the phone system. He spoke briefly with an officer on watch, who told him no, that his department did not keep records of boats in the fishery; only violators had names. And Johnathan clearly had obeyed the rules. Not for the first time, Russell wished every commercial fishing boat—and not just the Bering Sea crabbing boats—carried VMS (Vehicle Monitoring Systems), which were global positioning systems that transmitted a crab boat's geographic position at all times to federal National Marine Fisheries's computers in Washington, D.C. But no such luck.

Russell headed west-southwest and continually scanned the dark horizon for a light. His gut told him Johnathan was heading toward Augustine Island and the Shelikof Strait.

The Greater the Greed
the Faster the Pace

Andy

The telephone has not rung, which probably means that Russell is out of contact in the Inlet. And he has not found Johnathan. Sabrina is asleep and I brew a pot of coffee, which I carry out to the back porch. Today is going to be hot with plenty of humidity. The air is heavy and the sun, recently risen, is already mean with shimmering intensity. It is peculiar of me to go from a working life on the Bering Sea, where the temperatures go well below zero, to the summer heat of southern Indiana. I do not know which I like better and am glad I can have both.

That reminds me of the conundrum that Johnathan faces. I do too, but to a far smaller degree. It is that he will never leave the sea. I already have left it in my mind; but my heart refuses to follow. Johnathan's soul would be robbed of its sustenance without the ocean, a boat to work on, and crabs and salmon to catch. He would become someone different from what he is now, someone neither he nor I know. And yet staying on the sea could well kill him. The odds of survival never lengthen on the Bering Sea as the years go by. The equation for Johnathan (and anyone who tests the fates on the sea) becomes existential. Do you stop what you love to stay alive? Or do you continue to do what you love even if it kills you? It is a question of what a life is worth. I swear John would rather be dead.

The same quandaries do not preoccupy me. And for that I can thank Sabrina, who gave me a life that I love away from the sea. Our parents told us that Sabrina and I met when we were kids; neither she nor I remember being neighbors in Homer or that we played together before her family moved outside of town. We did not see each other again until our teens; she was working as a chambermaid out at Land's End, the hotel that my grandfather owned. My brothers and I knew who she was. I did not ask her out on dates, and her parents probably would not have let her go out with me. The Hillstrand boys had bad reputations and there were fathers who would have locked up their daughters rather than have them go out with any of us. We met again when we were in our twenties; she had given birth to Chelsey, who was around two when Johnathan's girlfriend, Tammy, introduced us at a party. It was love at first sight. What could have ended as a one-night stand grew into a solid marriage.

Sabrina was working as a real estate agent at the time. Her father, LeRoy, was a developer subdividing land and her mother, Rita, was the president of a Homer real estate office. Her family had nothing to do with fishing or the sea. In Homer, that was unusual. The differences in upbringing intrigued us both and brought us closer together. I would spend the night with her and sneak out the window before the babysitter arrived in the morning. One day, she asked me why I was sneaking out. We were married not long after.

Marriage did not change me and that led to trouble. I went on with my life much as before, working for my dad on the *Time*

Bandit. As if we were both still single, Sabrina and I hung out in bars and drank to see how plastered we could get. I would call her on the way home from the boat, drunk, slurring my words. I knew what she was thinking. But it would be too easy to say that alcohol nearly destroyed our marriage. Our lifestyle did it. We faced what hundreds of fishing couples face but fail to overcome.

Crab fishing gave me a sense of adventure. Nobody could tell me what to do. I was strictly my own man out there. That kind of thinking did not leave much room for Sabrina. It was the opposite of sharing. I could not talk to her about my life. I was not certain what I could say. I had my life and she was the landside part of it, the unadventurous, unexciting, routine part of it. She was not at the center of us together because there was no center; there was fishing and *after* fishing. That made her feel lonely and resentful of fishing, of my fishing family, and of the fisherman in me. She buried her resentments in booze. I stopped talking about fishing, about the risks, the dangers, the thrills. We had nothing to talk about, except that we had everything to talk about.

Sabrina could tell you what that life was like. When a boat broke or went down, she was in the circle of wives who called and talked continually. In that sense, it was as old as men going down to the sea. She knew whom to call. When Clark Sparks was lost overboard in New England, the boat's skipper, Thorn Tasker, asked her if she would call Clark's mom. He did not know to call anyone else but Sabrina. That was the worst phone call she ever made. Life for the women ashore was a series of calls. We talked through a marine operator and we would have to say "over" and "over-and-out." Anyone could listen in. People got divorces over the radio; nothing was private. That radio grew into a nightmare for us working on the boat. We did not want any attachment to the land. We hated when wives and girlfriends called with nothing to say except "Hello" and "How are you?" The last word we wanted to hear was about a drowning or another boat going down. The wives would call about that but we usually knew anyway, and we did not want to know from them. We would brush off catastrophe. We could not let ourselves get emotional, or else we would be basket cases all the time. We had to finish what we were doing and could not stop and mourn a tragedy.

Sabrina knew and respected that code but other women did not, or simply ignored it. She was like a den mother to them. Johnathan had a sequence of girlfriends who called her up all the time. "Have you heard from him? Is he okay?" Sabrina would tell them, "Chill out. If they are going to call you, they will." She had to teach them to go with the flow, not to be rigid, and to be open-minded. Sabrina had started out very rigid but she learned to let it go. Otherwise, she would still be tilting at windmills.

One time, Sabrina visited Dutch in the middle of a blizzard, and the temperature was 30 below zero. At that time I was working on a catcher processor called the *Optimist Prime*. Sabrina and I had come to an agreement that I could not be gone more than sixty days. After two months' separation, I either had to go home or Sabrina had to come to where I was working. I had been gone for three months and we had a four-month-old baby, Cassie. Sabrina thought she had landed in Hell. I was a lowly deckhand and I had to ask the captain if I could go to town. I got off at 8:30 in the evenings, went to the Grand Aleutian hotel, where Sabrina was staying with the baby, spent a couple of hours with her, went back to the boat, and after several nights, I was nearly dead with fatigue. I asked her, "Why don't you come out on the boat with the baby?"

The boat was anchored in the middle of Dutch harbor. One of my buddies took a skiff to pick up her and the baby at the dock.

She was out in the middle of the harbor with an infant in her arms praying for her life; the baby was screaming for hers. The skiff motor died. Sabrina had met the guy in the skiff minutes before and did not know whether to trust him. He started the engine, but the motor kept dying. At last, she reached the boat and she handed up our new baby to me. She spent a few days out there, more days than she would have liked, I think, but she did not want to take that skiff back to the dock.

As a fisherman on the Bering, I have to look my own mortality square in the eye not only for myself but for Sabrina and the girls. Sabrina had to be ready to lose me and be okay with that. Otherwise, she would be a nervous wreck. People ask her, "Aren't you worried about him out there?"

"No," she replies. "I had to turn that over to God. I had to let it go."

But the strain persisted. You cannot love someone and just let go the worry that he may die in a profession where dying is very real. You can learn to live with that reality. Like the time I was on the *Polar Star*, an eighty-six-footer. Sabrina got a telephone call that my boat had sunk. She did not believe that to be true. For some reason, she told herself, "That's wrong." If my boat went down, she knew the Coast Guard would have called her. She waited and worried. I had heard a Mayday that identified my boat as sunk. I looked around. *We're not sinking.* It was just confusion. A second boat named *Polar Star* had indeed sunk.

Sabrina may have put worry behind her, while living with the worst-case scenarios. She cannot walk around thinking I can die at any minute. It would be an unacceptable way to live. On TV she sees the wives of soldiers in Iraq. Those women say good-bye to their husbands and cry like they have already lost them. Sabrina could be doing the same thing every time I go away. She did, too, for a while. She would act brave and strong when I would leave. When she was alone, she would cry. People asked her how she did it. She answered them. "I just do it."

She did not blame her drinking on me, but the truth was, she hid her emotions in a bottle because of my inability to share mine and because we were both silently trying to spare each other of what we were really feeling. She grew up drinking and was an alcoholic when we met, and so was I and Johnathan and our dad. The Hillstrand men were not known for their social drinking; our DNA is soaked in alcohol.

For Sabrina and me, drinking went abruptly from all *to* nothing. We stopped together and started to change our lives after she made a conscious decision to leave the life of a fisherman's wife. The self-destructiveness had reached into her soul. She determined not to live a life anymore in bars, surrounded by oblivion, drinking, staying up, fights, disruptions, and tension. Together, we learned how to communicate better—and all that.

But by its nature, my life was disruptive and for Sabrina, as it is for all other fishing wives, it created challenges for us to overcome. To an extent, fishing wives see their husbands off, wait for them to come home, and then a big reunion celebrates their return. Distance does make the heart grow fonder but only up to a point. I would go home, and I automatically assumed that I was the head of the household. I sat in the easy chair and took command of the TV remote control. But Sabrina was used to making the decisions at home. She did not call the boat to say the car broke down, what do I do? She fixed it. Women are the natural organizers and the captains of the house. I was the captain of the ship out on the Bering Sea. I would come home and think I automatically was the captain of the house, too. Who was the captain? We sat down together and agreed. "OK, you be in charge of this, and I'll be in charge of that." Sabrina and I ended up asking, "How important is being in charge anyway? Why do I have to play it only my way?" It's a constant balancing act.

Ten years of marriage went by before we spent more than sixty days in a row together. There was always another opening: salmon, herring, crab. And I worked at the whim of my dad. In American society everyone, on paper at least, is free to do what he wants to do and be what she wants to be. In marriage, the other person had to change. But when both people wanted the other person to change, friction and failure were the result. Sabrina had her own income. She had started a real estate company and worked as a bartender and waitress and a journalist for the Homer *Tribune*. She ran a donut shop until donuts made her sick when she was pregnant. I tried to run the shop for a while, but it was destroying me. I learned that she did not need me. We had to work out who was in charge and when and what were our individual responsibilities. Learning to work as a team was the hardest and most rewarding work I have ever done, or will ever do, because we worked side by side.

Sabrina comes out on the porch where I am sitting with a cup in hand. She sits down and looks at me.

"Did you sleep?" she asks.

"A little," I replied.

"What would you like to do about Johnathan?"

"What can I do?"

She stares in the direction of the horse ring. "It's still dark there," she says, referring to the three-hour time difference between Indiana and Alaska.

"You mean the Coast Guard?"

"Would it do any good for you to fly up there?"

I think about that. I can tell that she is worried about Johnathan, too. She is used to not showing her concern. She has had years of practice. "Not until Russ calls," I tell her. "I think that's what worries me, that I can't do anything but sit here and worry."

She laughs softly and goes inside.

Moments like these lead me to introspection, which is something I usually manage to avoid. As I walk over to the barn to check on Rio and the other horses, I think about change. For instance, one of the changes I enjoy, I am able to live thousands of miles from the *Time Bandit* and the Bering Sea fishing grounds. But not all the changes in the last ten years or so have been as welcome. Commercial fishermen like Johnathan and me are many things: We are born optimists; we are fierce competitors; we are hard workers and harder to lead than a herd of cats. Above everything, we can't tolerate change, despite its inevitability. Take the change that came to Alaskan crab fishing. We are still trying to get comfortable with that.

In 1976, with the passage of the Magnuson-Stevens Fisheries Conservation and Management Act, and the international fishing boundary expanded from 12 to 200 miles. Effectively, the act Americanized Alaskan fisheries. Without the Russians and the Japanese ships scooping crabs in tons aboard their industrial boats, Alaskan fishermen were finally left alone to catch what belonged to the people of Alaska. This was the good news. The bad news was that a new and alarming lethality crept into an industry that was already dangerous enough.

From the start, the crab catch was organized around *The Derby*, jargon for "open access." I loved the Derby, which had a wild anarchy of the kind that is not much sanctioned in America anymore, on the sea or off. The game was every man for himself, a virtual free-for-all, with no regulation once the starting gun went off, and it suited my nature, which probably says more about me than I should admit. Put another way, the Derby was like a cattle drive on the sea, from the days of the Chisholm Trail, when real cowboys herded their longhorns to the railheads.

Crews like ours on *Time Bandit* worked without sleep in all weather and seas to catch as many crabs in an allotted time as our holds would take and our bodies would allow. Johnathan and I, who know better than to take unnecessary risks at sea, went ahead anyway in search of the *red gold* that we call king crabs. Secrecy was the guiding rule. No boat captain ever told another captain about his hot spots, where he reliably would find crabs year after year. The crabs shifted their grounds, and no one spoke over the single sideband what their prospect pots showed or where they were successful. Meanwhile, ships were going down at a rate that everyone knew was unacceptable, even criminal, and yet no one knew what could be done to stop it. No one was really even certain why.

The Derby created the dawning of a perfect storm for Alaskan fishermen. Whether anyone ever meant the crab fishery to become a breakneck race against time, elements, and the fishing of a species of sea creature that, while it does not swim, moves freely over the sea floor, the circumstances began to kill men. Any captain with a license and a boat, no matter what size or concern of its captain for safety, could enter the Derby just by showing up. Boats went out on the Bering Sea that did not have the seaworthiness to handle the wind and weather. The State of Alaska's Department of Fish & Game set catch limits to protect the long-term health of the crabs; but Fish & Game, acknowledging the cussedness of fishermen, let them take care of their own long-term health, which was something that the fishermen clearly would show themselves incapable of doing.

The Derby frenzy started each year, usually in September, on a precise day at an exact minute. Aware that the season might last only fifty-two hours, the fishermen worked ceaselessly and took alarming risks to plug their holds. In some years, forecasts of storms on the Bering forced Fish & Game to delay the opening for the protection of fishermen who would simply ignore their better judgment to remain in port and face whatever the Bering Sea had to throw at them. The catch was like sand dropping through an hourglass. Fish & Game continually estimated the catch according to the numbers and sizes of the licensed boats and the tonnage of their deliveries to the processors. They knew within hours when the fleet would reach the preset limit, and an announcement over single sideband signaled a day and an exact time of the season's end. The boat crews worked with increased fury, knowing the minutes were ticking down. Tired, aching, and groggy, crews and captains made fatal mistakes.

Unwittingly, the federal government made a bad situation even more dangerous with an unintentional consequence. The National Marine Fisheries Service, a part of the National Oceanic and Atmospheric Administration (NOAA), invited crab fishermen to reinvest what they otherwise would have paid in taxes in capital construction. At first, boat owners used the tax money to rebuild their vessels. They added new technologies that increased their speed and the tonnage of the catch. With their existing vessels updated, the captains plowed more tax-free money in two, three, five, or eight *new* boats that they designed to ply seas in any weather, with larger holds for greater tonnages of crabs. They built in booms for sodium lights, allowing them to work night and day, and decks strong enough to hold megatons of pots.

This overcapitalization created a frenzy of too many boats with larger capacities racing for the same limit of crab. Captains were stacking more weight on their decks than the boats were designed to carry; stability suffered, and boats and lives were lost. Accidents began to alarm officials at the Alaska Fish & Game. Boat captains determined the numbers and sizes of the pots they carried on deck. Pots, of course, are a blessing *and* a curse. For the deckhands and boat owners, they trap the crabs that fill our pockets with cash. But they can also kill us. Pots like the ones we carry on *Time Bandit* can slam against the deck with 30,000 foot-pounds of energy; we do not wear steel-toed safety shoes because the force of a falling pot is greater than the steel plate in the shoes can withstand, and the plate would cut flesh and bone like a scalpel.

On the deck, the pots swing at the end of the crane hook above the deckhands' heads. The greater the greed, the faster the pace. The rhythm of the crew working together cannot be accelerated beyond the speed of the slowest man or the most complicated task without creating further risks. The pots can slide like runaway trains along wooden deck boards slick with ice and crab slime. In icy conditions, a loose pot can take down a crewman without warning or crush him against the rail or the wave wall or any number of steel surfaces near the deck. They can smash fingers and snap limbs in an instant of inattention and, when attached to three buoys at the end of 33-fathom "shots" of three-quarter-inch line, they possess the terrifying potential of dragging a crewman overboard down into the depths of the Bering Sea.

The enormous collective weight of the pots when stacked on the deck raises a boat's center of gravity and thereby creates a continuing threat to the entire boat. Too much weight destabilized and sank boats during the Derby with an alarming regularity. Adding a further and even more unpredictable element of instability, in the Bering Sea ice forms in thick sheets on deck and the pots. This factor makes the difference, often, between safety and disaster. The ice can build up with alarming speed. The initial weight of ice a foot thick on the decks causes a boat like *Time Bandit* to push bluntly into the bow waves, and this in turn throws cascades of salt water and spray on the deck and forepeak. This spray sometimes turns to ice *in the air*, falling to deck in frozen drops with the rattle of marbles in a tin can. Soon, the boat turns sluggish at the wheel and refuses even to respond. With the ice weight now added to the pot weight and with the boat sluggish, one wave can capsize the boat.

When a boat is "making ice," the crew must be prepared to hit the deck, literally, with sledgehammers, baseball bats, axes, and lengths of pipe to break up. The work is slow and hard. Frostbitten ears and hands are not uncommon. The ice is pitched overboard or shoved out a scuttle. Breaking ice is a race against time. Sometimes, keeping even with the new ice is all that a crew can do. The crew knows the importance of getting ice off the boat, and few seriously complain when I tell them to get at it.

Another hazard peculiar to crabbing boats, the crab tanks can detract immeasurably from the boats' stability. These tanks are filled with water to keep the crabs alive until they are delivered to the processors. Pumps must continually replenish the seawater in the tanks, and if for some reason the pumps fail, the water in the tanks may slosh from one side to another and destabilize the boat. That may have happened to Cache Seel and his ninety-two-foot crabber *Big Valley* in January 2005, while surrounded by other crab boats seventy miles off the Pribilof Island of St. Paul's.

The *Big Valley* was caught in the trough between waves twelve to fifteen feet high when without warning a twenty-eight-foot rogue wave turned the boat on its side 60 to 70 degrees. In his bunk, Seel was flipped nearly vertical; the engines quit and the generators shut down. In the pitch dark he struggled into his survival suit and went to aid another crewman crying for help. On deck another crewman deployed a life raft, which howling winds blew away. The deck tipped 90 degrees within two minutes and threw two crewmen into the icy waters with their survival suits in their hands. The boat gradually rolled and settled about two-thirds upside down. The rolling chocks, fins that run along either side of a keel from the stern forward and are normally underwater, were exposed to the air. Now a cascade of events pointed in a single direction. The other four crewmen walked along the hull as the boat rolled. Seel ended up near the stern in the water. Enough of the boat was still afloat for him to cling to a protruding fixture on the hull. But as the boat settled down farther in the water, waves broke over the hull. Seel could not see his crewmates in the dark but he could hear them yelling that the EPIRB emergency beacon had floated free. For the next hour and a half, he held on, as higher waves washed over the upturned hull. The boat sank deeper into the water, and Seel finally had to let go. For the next twenty minutes, he swam free of the boat until he saw a white strobe light beaming from a raft. After thirty minutes more swimming, he climbed into the raft to safety, vomited seawater, and waited for the Coast Guard to hoist him into a helicopter two hours later.

Inspectors later determined, based on speculation and Seel's recollection of events, that "free surface," which describes slack water in the boat's compartments, was either full of water or completely empty. A pump had failed in the crab hold and the water was slack; a cutlass bearing broke and water flooded the engine room; or water poured through doors that were not secured in the rear lazarette. Water sloshed around inside the boat, and the weight moved to one side as the boat rocked with the actions of the waves in the trough. At some point the side-to-side motion grew extreme. The boat could not recover from a roll, and went over.

That was the end of *Big Valley*, but the sea was the killer only as an instrument of man's stupidity. Usually this is the case, although no one wants to talk about stupidity leading to the deaths of crewmen. We are aware of the dangers we face, and we are not afraid. Most of the time, we work without a thought of drowning or freezing to death. We fishermen are not especially brave but we have a healthy capacity to deceive ourselves. Consider our rates of survival against other dangerous jobs. In 2006 the U.S. Bureau of Labor Statistics ranked commercial fishing in general as the work with the highest fatality rate in America with 141.7 fatalities per 100,000, almost thirty times that of an average industrial worker. And the Bureau lists Alaskan waters and in particular the Bering Sea, which has claimed 2,066 lives since records were first kept, as far more dangerous still.

But you are never the one who is going to die, until the night you wake up and men are screaming and the engine room is half full of water, and suddenly you are in the water, alarms going off, and you are in shock. You tell yourself, "I don't believe this is happening to *me*." Five minutes later, you are crab food. You cannot allow yourself ever to think you are going to be the one who dies. That is what, I suppose, keeps us sane. It is also what molds our character. A slip, a careless instant, a spasm of hand movements of the crane operator on his controls and someone on deck can die. The sea rocks and heaves the deck under our boots. Standing upright without holding on takes constant effort, and when a crewman is sorting crabs or working with buoy lines— indeed, any of the tasks on the deck—his life is at risk. Waves of water crash over the bow. The boat rolls, starboard to port, often with a heave from the stern, corkscrewing crewmen off balance and toward the rails. At any instant, a twisted ankle, an unexpected rogue wave, a slip on fish guts, a crab scuttling over the deck, or plates of ice, and a crewman can go to his death. It can happen fast. No wonder we do not grow up. If we did, we would have no choice but to quit crabbing.

We think of ourselves as neither crazy nor foolish. Other people can think that, but it is a luxury we do not acknowledge. We are men working at our chosen profession. Every fisherman knows what kills. We understand that if we enter the water unprotected, we are probably as good as dead. A crewman will be irretrievably wounded by hypothermia in four or five minutes if he is not wearing a survival suit when he enters the Bering Sea. His extremities will quickly go numb as his body struggles to protect its central core, and he will die when his heart reaches 86 degrees Fahrenheit. We are not afraid of the sea; we are *terrified* of the water.

In our world of denial, we turn away from certain risks as part of the cost of crabbing. But denial is more complicated than that. Some fishermen invite their own destruction. Captain Ahab lives on the Bering Sea! Men bring about their own peril through greed, complacency, and desperation. The same stupid motives apply whether men are racing NASCAR or picking stocks and bonds. A person who is desperate for money *will* act stupid. Any crabber who says he has never known desperation is flat-out lying. Anything I ever did in desperation turned out wrong, like it did with the *Perfect Storm* guys, whom no one forced into that storm. They had lost refrigeration and chose to run for the money. And only when they were in peril did they realize that all the money in the world was not worth dying for. I should not criticize them for what they did. The stresses at sea can make fools of men. Out on the Bering, the crew on deck is looking up at me making decisions in the wheelhouse, and I see the faces of their wives and kids looking back at me too. I have to make them money, *and* I must bring them home alive. I may worry about drowning, dying in a ship's fire, or from a falling pot, and making it back to port, for whatever good worrying will do, but I *have* to make money for my crew. On the sea, my back is to the wall. One bad season, I can borrow to make ends meet; after two bad seasons in a row, I am close to going under. Three bad, and I go directly to jail without passing go; I am back twenty years working the deck where I started. Either way, I have lost my dream. And *that* thought alone can lead to disaster.

At last, Alaska Fish & Game determined that something had to make crabbing safer, and in the process, they decided to give the crab fishery a new structure to sustain its health over the long term. They called their plan "rationalization." It was not an entirely new concept, but it had never been applied to crabbing. My brother and I hate the new system as it is unfair and stacked in favor of the Alaskan natives and the giant processors. Begrudgingly, we will say that Alaska manages its fisheries fairly well. Each year, the North Pacific Council Management, which includes Alaska Fish & Game and the National Fisheries Service, accesses the crab stocks in the Bering Sea—how many are out there, how many are males, females, and juveniles. Crabs, the state reminds us fishermen correctly, are a shared resource that does not belong to us. Crabs belong to the 700,000-plus people of Alaska. The state, in setting up the new regulations for crab, assigned each boat an IFQ based on each boat's average catch over the previous five years; the owner then was allowed either to lease his quota to another fisherman for half the profit or fish for the quota himself for full profit over an extended time.

The state arrived at each IFQ, expressed in a percentage of the total catch limit, by removing the best and worst year's catch of each individual boat between 1998 and 2002, and averaging what remained. The state eliminated from IFQs the fishery boats with averages below a set minimum. In other words, boats had to be real crabbers and not part of the mob that went to the Derby now and then. *Time Bandit* received an initial IFQ of 90,000 pounds of king crab and an original IFQ of 225,000 pounds of opilio crab, less 50,000 pounds that we lease out each year.

In 2005, the first year of rationalization, we decided to sit back and just fish our own quota. We should have leased other crabbers' quota, too. In the 2006–2007 crab season we acquired extra quota, but only so much was available. Ten percent of our catch goes automatically to the native Alaskans. If we lease quotas, we have to give 50 percent of what we catch for opilio and about 70 percent for king to the lease owners. With the new system of IFQs, we fishermen are risking our lives catching crabs for one half or one third of what it is really worth.

We need a sixth crewman—an accountant.

After rationalization, pressures on us remained, of course, in spite of the relative sanity created by the new system. Diesel fuel costs (from $1.50 per gallon in 2005 to $3.10 in 2007) created one constant pressure. With fuel costs rising, fishermen do not dawdle on the Bering. The competition still spurs the fishermen to desperate lengths, as before. Fish & Game is not quite willing to accept responsibility for accidents at sea, which remain as high as ever. Anyone can read anything in statistics, and safety looks good on paper, but from where I sit in the wheelhouse of *Time Bandit*, safety will always be a mixed bag. What can ever prevent pitfalls on the deck floor, the pots, the launcher, the picking hook that swings through the air, the heaving deck, the open hatches to the holds where a crewman easily can crack an ankle bone or break a leg with a single off-balance misstep or fall through the hatch twenty feet to the bottom of the fish hold? Or what safety measure will ever stop a heavy steel deck door from slamming shut on a leg with the shift of the boat in a heavy sea? Last year the deck door slammed on a crewman's lower leg. He came up to me later and said, "I thought it was cool that my leg was still attached when I looked at it; it felt like scissors cutting it in two."

Comparatively, crabbing has grown into a less deadly job on a still-violent and still-injurious sea. We are guaranteed to catch crabs. We know where to find them, year after year, with the use of plotters and knowledge of their migratory habits. We catch 225,000 pounds of opilio without fail under rationalization. We try not to catch a single pound more. We never catch less. And while we are given the time, we rarely take the time to soak the pots and rest the crew. Time is money. I might feel comfortable telling fishermen in port where to find crabs, whereas my lips were sealed before. That removes an element of mystery from the process and, some say, it may not qualify as fishing anymore. It's more like *catching*. I disagree. We are guaranteed money under rationalization, but nothing else. Will crab fishing become nothing more than a numbers game? Must the fleet become corporate in order to survive? Probably so.

No wonder what we fear from rationalization is the future.

Alaska does not enjoy the luxury of diverse industries, like Washington and Oregon, which also are home ports for Alaskan crabbing boats. Alaska has oil on the North Slope and fishing in the Bering Sea. The oil aside, the state consists of remote communities that depend on fishing for their livelihoods. Unemployed workers cannot simply drive across town for a job at Boeing or Microsoft, as they might be able to do in Seattle. Without fishing, they have few if any real alternatives. When the oil is depleted on the Slope, the state will have to rely on fishing for employment, which means jobs on *land* as well as on the sea.

When Fish & Game first considered the rationalization of

crabbing, they looked to stabilize the fishery over the long term. The Derby had brought jobs to places like Dutch Harbor in the short run; rationalization, by reducing the catch and the fleet, reduced the number of jobs. Before rationalization, more than 357 boats with 1,500 fished for king and opilio crabs. Dutch Harbor swung from boom to bust by the month. Boat captains and processors flew workers in. When their work was done, they flew them out. Nobody stayed for long.

Now, under rationalization, 80 boats catch their crab quotas with the help of about 400 crewmen. Workers in the canneries can be assured that their work will be steady through most of the year. The catch is delivered on an orderly schedule. The big processors have turned dorms for their workers into living quarters for men and their families. Roads are paved on Unalaska for the first time. Schools are growing, and decent public facilities have sprung up. Dutch is no longer a camp with a couple of saloons. But where does any of that leave the fishermen?

We crabbers crab with good reason. We want to know why we cannot sell our total catch to any processor who offers us the highest price. That was how it used to be. Now, we can sell only ten percent of our catch on open market. We must deliver the rest to a contracted processor who tells us what he will pay us per pound. Selling 100 percent in an open market, isn't that the American way?

As matters stand, we fishermen receive an average of $4.20 ($3.85 in 2006) for each red king crab we take to the processor. That may not seem like much given our efforts and the risks. But we have nothing to say about the price. The world market determines that. Russian and Norwegian boats harvest crabs in the Barents Sea at a rate that is flooding the markets and driving prices down. Consumers of crab care about what they spend, of course. Crab meat is an expensive delicacy. If a consumer can buy Russian king crab at Costco for $11 or $12 a pound, why should he pay more for Alaskan king crab, even if Alaskan crab is demonstrably better processed and prepared? With the Russians and Norwegians sweeping the Barents Sea clean, our share of Bering Sea's crab is declining on the world market. Last year, the Alaskan fleet brought in 15.5 million pounds of king crab. That quota was down about 15 percent from the year before to guarantee the health of the crab stocks. By contrast, Russia crabbers owned up to catching 33 million pounds in the Barents Sea, but they cheat on statistics. Their real catch was probably double what they reported.

We whine about price, but as long as Alaska supplies only a small percentage of the rapidly increasing volume in markets like Japan and the United States, Alaskan fishermen and processors will have little to say about the market supply and virtually nothing to say about the price of its king crab.

The state is now encouraging us crabbers to join co-ops. *Time Bandit* is a member of one out of its own self-interest. If we catch more crabs than the limit our IFQs allow, instead of paying a fine, or worse, dumping the crabs back into the sea, other boats in our co-op that have not yet fished can account for our excess, which they can sell without catching. The state would like us to go even further with our co-ops by joining forces with the processors in true cooperation. We are not yet ready to take that step. It will never work; as we see it, cooperation would be like putting a fox in the henhouse.

We are afraid of becoming hourly salaried workers with the adventure, traditions, and romance of crabbing buried under pages of quotas and rules and regulations. We do not want to be part of a bureaucracy. We do not sit well on committees and at meetings around boardroom tables. We are men who work with our hands. Debates are meant for bars. We work harder in short bursts than any other laborers in America. We have seen what industry and cooperatives did to farmers. Fishermen are independent, ornery, and wary of change. We sense that once we let go, we will lose ourselves. What worries us crabbers is how quickly our way of life might simply disappear.

Have we reached the last frontier? Yes. The old ways are disappearing in a blur of speed. Yet fishermen hold on to what only God can change. As long as we fish for crabs, nothing can diminish the dangers inherent in our work. Nothing will change the winds and the sea. The Bering, then, is our last frontier. It is our Wild West, our Lonesome Dove, played out on waves.

I Fear What Lives
Under the Sea

Johnathan

The sea is rougher now, and *Fishing Fever* is in the troughs. I have no power to jog the boat into the sea. With a motor I could take the waves bow-on, but without power she is turned broadside in the troughs. The ride is rough; the boat is light and no match for the swells. The tide has turned against the wind. The seas are fifteen or sixteen feet, not yet of a height that threatens to capsize me, but they are nearly half as high as my boat's length. I am a little worried.

I strip down in order to layer warmer clothes. I must be ready for anything. I am standing on the floor in the wheelhouse in my underpants when suddenly I start to laugh. This is a funny, not a psychotic, laugh, although either would be appropriate. I have not thought about this in years, but once, not too long ago, I was staying on the thirtieth floor of a hotel on the opposite side of the casino on the Las Vegas Strip. I ordered lunch from room service. When I finished eating, I pulled back the covers and went back to bed. I must have slept for four or five hours. The clock said it was the late afternoon and downstairs the casino would be coming to life with suckers just like me. I like to gamble; it is a pleasure, not a need. I like the action and the life. The lunch leavings smelled, and I pushed the cart out the door into the hall. I was turning around when I heard the door click. I straightened up like I had heard a shot. I was standing on the carpeted hallway in my tightie-whities, nothing but pure WalMart BVDs. I was thinking, *If I only wore boxers!* I saw no alternative to taking an elevator to the ground floor. I walked through the casino, all across the casino to the other side. People did not know what to think. They were like, "What the fuck? Just look at that. They took everything from him but his underpants."

I kept my eyes straight ahead, my hands folded like I was going to communion. At the front desk the line stretched, it seemed at the time, from here to eternity. I got in the rear, and waited. I looked up at the ceiling. Remember when you were a kid and had nightmares about going to school in your underwear and you would wake up screaming? That was happening. We inched forward, and at last I was talking to an employee, who glanced over the counter and with admirable self-control did not give a single hint of anything out of the ordinary. I asked for a new card key. I explained the circumstance.

She was a cold bitch. She asked me, "How do we know it's you? Do you have an I.D., *sir*?"

I said, "Come on, man."

Security on either elbow escorted me back to my room.

A plug of Copenhagen soothes me now. On the shelf in the wheelhouse sits a bottle of Chantix that is supposed to help me stop smoking. The pills work. That is why I do not take them. With Chantix I do not feel like smoking or anything else that is bad for me, like eating greasy McDonald's. You would be surprised how bad that little sonofabitch gallbladder can make you feel. You do not actually need one either. Chantix makes me feel like shit. I might as well take diet pills.

In seas like these, I can get seasick. In the crab season, I almost always puke the first night out. I am feeling like doing that now. My stomach is queasy, and I am half prepared to run for the head, but *Fishing Fever* has no head; I have the whole wide sea to hurl in. I lie down on the bunk and roll with the waves. Normally this calms my stomach, but right now the motion of the waves is not what is giving me butterflies. A boat can be more relaxing than anything else when everything is going right. When it is like now, anxiety can churn my guts. There is nothing I can do, which makes the queasy feeling only worse.

In the dark, I distract myself by thinking of what I am not afraid of. I do not fear heights; in fact, I love to freefall from airplanes. I do not fear the sea, though I have been afraid *on* the sea. One night last year in the king crab season, a 100-foot rogue wave with a 30-foot whitewater "viper" slammed into *Time Bandit. That* frightened me beyond the measure of I-thought-we-were-done-for. Andy was in the captain's chair and I was in my stateroom when a wave hit us from behind. I did not know what was happening. Everything was falling. I could not reach the ladder to the engine room. Then that huge rogue, following behind that wave, punched us upright. Andy told me later that the impact tossed him up to the ceiling. It threw the microwave right through the galley door. It tore the refrigerator and stove off their bolts. We were sixty feet under the water. The whole boat was shuddering—*dut dut dut dut.* The engines sputtered. I thought it was over. I did not see how we could *not* go over. This was the kind of wave that takes out small villages. No one onboard said a word. We collected like crows up in the wheelhouse. Andy was clutching the wheel. I thought, *We are going to see Davy Jones.*

More than anything, more than rogues, I fear what lives *under* the sea. I used to work, when I was not fishing, as a commercial diver, mostly pulling propellers. I would use regular scuba gear and wear a dry suit. I used wrenches and hammers and welding equipment, whatever was needed to do the job. I was happy with this work, but then I saw the movie *Jaws*, and the underwater world was never again the same for me.

One time I was working to repair a shaft about twenty feet under the water when I noticed that a sea lion was swimming around me. I imagined that he wanted to see what was up. I watched him out of the corner of my eye as I worked. Suddenly, he swam straight at me, grabbed my shoulder with his teeth, and pulled me through the water. I knew exactly the feeling of being in a shark's mouth. I kicked loose of him and came straight up to the surface. My eyeballs were big as saucers.

I only dove twice more after that, but I watched my back in a big way. Now I am afraid of sea lions even when I am *not* under the water. They congregate in Kodiak harbor because people feed them off the dock. A man was sitting with his ass over the pier, and a sea lion grabbed him and took a big chunk out. He got his gun and shot the sea lion dead, and the police arrested him. Does that make sense to you? If a bear comes into town and starts eating your kids, you shoot him, don't you? What's so different about sea lions eating ass?

Thanks to the movie *Jaws*, I am more scared of sharks than I am of drowning. I was long-lining off the East Coast once when a fifteen-foot blue shark swam up to the transom. At the time, I was drinking a cup of coffee. He looked up at the transom. He scared the shit out of me. I hit him on the head with the cup, which fell into the water, and he ate it. I *wanted my cup back*. No shark was going to take it without a fight. The shark followed the boat for three days looking, I supposed, either for more coffee cups or for a chance to eat me. I hooked up a big bait bag on a grapple, and the shark grabbed that grapple hook with all the power in its jaws. I fought him on a line for six hours. And then I got tired and I dragged him to death at eight knots. At the dock, I opened his gut with a knife. My coffee cup fell out with a broken handle. I glued the handle back on and called it even with the shark. I have every reason to believe that if he ate my coffee cup he would have eaten me if I had fallen overboard.

I also do not like killer whales, which swim in pods in Alaskan waters. I have seen what they do to creatures smaller than they are. They throw sea otters up in the air like eating popcorn. They would probably not *intend* to eat me, a man, but what would that matter if they mistook me for a sea otter? Tourists might shake their heads if they knew that an orca had eaten a human. But if they heard that an orca had eaten a sea otter, they would demand action. Nothing on or under the ocean is cuter than a sea otter. They are like puppies. . . . you could make slippers out of them. But they eat every clam and every crab from the shore to ten miles out to sea and then they move somewhere else and do the same thing there. Orcas and sea otters, I say, are a balance of nature. Orcas and me, not so much.

And last of all, I am afraid of marriage. That is why I never came close or met the right woman. A relationship with a woman should grow and not be like a roller coaster ride. Getting married is not going to make it smoother. Like I say, when I drink, I drink. When I work, I work. When I am with a lady, I'm with that lady. I treat ladies real good. I treat boats good, too. I would have to work at a marriage, and crabbers like me are working too hard at fishing to have something worthwhile left for marriage. Besides, crabbers say, "You don't lose your wife, you lose your turn."

Here is what happens: You come home from fishing after three months to find your wife in the bar, and that is not good.

The fishing life is hard on them, too. I stayed with two women because we had babies together, and I put investments and stuff like houses I owned in their names, so it was *like* we were married. That ended our relationships as we had known them and would have ended our marriages. With the arrival of kids, there was no more sex on the kitchen table. All the romance went out the window. The babies slept in bed with us. I had to take their mother to a motel once a week for sex.

The irony of my own children is that they have brought me untold happiness. My daughter gave birth to my second grandchild, Tiana, last October. My son's wife had my first grandchild, Sawyer, last September. I became a double grandpa within a month, and am happy to say I am proud. I hope their parents do a better job of raising them than I did raising my children.

My son Scott had a tough childhood partly due to me being a fisherman. He hardly saw me for nine months out of the year. He lived in Homer with my Grandma Jo and in Idaho with my mother and with my stepfather Bob. Scott's mother was not around. When I was in town as he got older, he went with me on the boat, catching fish and tendering, and, more or less, he grew up on boats. He tells me how one of his first memories was tendering when he was five. At the time, his cousin Chelsey was on the boat, too. One morning, the crew and Andy and I were asleep when a boat came up to deliver salmon. Scott and Chelsey tried to wake us up, but Andy and I told them to go away. Without another word, they went up on deck and tied up the boat themselves.

I gave Scott tough love. He was fifteen, failing at school and into drugs. He totaled my truck. I told him he had to pay me. At the end of the summer, he had made $14,000; I took out $2,000 for the IRS and $8,000 for my truck. I told him, "Welcome to the real world."

To get his life in order as a teenager, I gave him two options: Go out fishing with me or straighten out by yourself. He quit school and went to sea with me. At the end of that year, I wanted him to return to school. He asked me if I would go back if I was making $14,000 a year when I was only fifteen? He fished with me and bounced boats for the next seven years. Fishing became a celebration for him. He never thought of the dangers. He turned himself into a working machine as a deckhand. The sun went up and went down, up and down, while he did nothing else but work. And he liked it. He liked the sea. It was an escape. For Scott fishing meant living the life of a rock star. When he walked into the bar and rang the bell and was throwing down $100 bills, life was cool.

Once at sea last year, we started out slow. The king crabs were not cooperating with *Time Bandit*'s timetable. We traveled east and north to a line approximating the area between Bristol Bay and the Bering Sea that had served us well the previous year. About two hours after leaving Dutch Harbor I started feeling seasick and gave the watch to Richard and went below. I lay down on my bunk, and before I could count to one hundred it was time for me to drive the porcelain bus. Once I puked, I felt fine. But I did not see the point of going back to the wheelhouse, and I went back to bed.

The next morning, we launched prospecting pots, and the deck routine went as usual. I rank the jobs on the deck according to risk and skill levels. Last year, Neal operated the crane with economy, precision, and speed; he always does. Neal on the hydros eases the minds of the deck crew. He works in a smooth rhythm. Nothing ever surprises him at the controls. The hydros may look easy to operate but they come with a cost of pain. Neal must stand at his station in the freezing cold and wet. He cannot move. His hands and feet freeze. He has had arthritis in his knuckles for years. In spite of the agony of the cold and discomfort of the wet, he has never laid a pot on a crewman's head or pinned one against a rail. He has reason to be proud of his skills. He never gets sloppy. One "oops" from him, and a crewmate can end up injured. Neal says little. He is a pro who stays out of the way. As a captain in the wheelhouse looking down on the deck, sometimes I wonder if he is even there. That is how good he is.

He is a jack of all trades. He knows woodworking, welding, and engine mechanics. He says often longingly that he would like to have been a fireman or an explosives man, like the ones who implode entire buildings. He might have made careers of them but he could never stand the nine to five. One time he sold furniture in a store. He quit soon after he started. He told me, "I don't like bosses."

He is also *Time Bandit*'s cook, and nobody gets in his way when he is working in the galley, which has less space perhaps than a kitchen in a small apartment, although with a grand view of the sea out a single porthole over the sink. Neal clearly enjoys cooking. Though he is not a great chef, his staples—eggs, pancakes, bacon, hash, spaghetti with meat sauce, etc.—are as good as they can get on a boat. He cooks roasts and other high-protein dishes that he can prepare in advance and puts in potatoes and vegetables at the last moment. His specialty is crab plucked from the sea and immersed in a large pot of seawater. He serves the delicacy with a brush of butter. When crab is on Neal's menu, which is not often, the crew never complains. He plans the timing of the meals, as best he can, around the schedule of the captain, for example, asking me when I estimate the crew will get a break between launching and lifting the pots.

The crew eats like starved beasts. No matter what or how

much, the food vanishes in minutes of silent gulping. The crew hardly comes up for air. A gallon of milk will disappear as quickly as the spout will pour. An enormous eighteen-pound roast beef, fresh from the oven, was reduced to bones last year at three in the morning. The men eat dessert from two-gallon containers of ice cream. Whatever is placed on the table is never enough, and though he knows that food for the crew is nothing but fuel, Neal still takes a measure of pride from cooking for them.

I take nothing for granted about what Neal achieves in the galley. The miracle is that he can cook anything on the Bering. The seas are rough all the time. If we can let go of a stationary, steadying object like a wall, counter, bed, or sink, for *five seconds* without falling off balance, we think of the sea as calm. It happens rarely. To cook in that shifting, topsy-turvy world requires Neal to rig the stove top with adjustable braces for pots and pans, and boiling water sloshes on the counter or floor anyway. One time a boiling pot went straight up in the air nearly to the ceiling. He has cooked bacon in twenty-footers. Scrambled eggs seemed easy; he would not attempt to cook an egg over-easy.

Last year, Neal brought onboard a month-old Jack Russell terrier puppy that he named Bandit, with a semicircle of brown around his left eye. Bandit was learning to coordinate his legs, and he moved around the boat less to the places he might have wanted to visit than according to the motion of the boat. He slept with Neal and played on the deck with live crabs. Richard and Shea trailed after him with newspapers when Neal notified them that it might be time for Bandit to "go poopoo."

Dogs at sea are an old tradition. Mine was named Jake, a mutt, part boxer, part lab, with evil white eyes. Jake weighed about 100 pounds. I took him fishing each year to Togiak in Bristol Bay. He would not go to the bathroom on the boat. I would go, "Come on, boy, you can do it," but he never did. He never sniffed crotch and was no ass sniffer either. He knew he was a dog. He was my buddy.

One time, Jake fell off the boat eight miles off Togiak. He had smelled the land. I did not notice that he was gone until much later. A fisherman named Larry Jones was following my boat three hours behind me. He saw what he thought was a seal. He looked closer. He said, "Sonofabitch, that's a weird-colored seal. That ain't no seal. That's a dog. That's Jake. What's he doing out here?"

Jake had treaded water for three hours. He was a lucky dog, and a pampered one. He had his own taxi account. When I would go out drinking in Homer, I would call Nick at Night, the cabdriver in town who would take Jake home. He had his own tab. Jake was fourteen when he died. It was tough on me. Two days after I lost him, I started crying, "Goddamned dog." He was just a dog, but I knew him for so long.

Once we started launching prospecting pots, everyone, including Bandit, went out on deck, with me the sole exception. Richard took charge of the bait station; he shoved through a mechanical grinder that amounted to tons of herring by the end of the season. He smelled of an evil overpowering stench of ground-up herring and fish puke that quickly permeated his rain gear, hair, and skin. Even his farts started to smell of rotted herring. Richard, who is as good as they come, filled the plastic bait boxes by fistfuls and gutted the cod with his knife, before clambering into each pot on the launcher to hook the baits on the pot's webbing—hundreds of times, over and over again. The bait station demands grinding stamina. Wrists, forearms, and hands ache and swell and chafe in the cold and ice.

Nimble Caveman, a crewman last year who shall go un-
named, scrambled on stacks of pots five high that rose from the
deck to the wheelhouse windows. The dangerous stack work required a delicate balancing act. Pots swung overhead on the end
of a picking hook on the bridle. Caveman guided their weight
and bulk into ordered rows, risking crushed hands and feet with
each pot that settled off the line. The boat heaved and wallowed
as if it were trying to throw Caveman into the sea. At any instant,
a rogue wave might have whacked the boat and unsettled his
footing high on the stack. If *Time Bandit* needed to come around
to rescue him, he would have been beyond saving by the time we
reached him. The safety line might have saved him, but there
never are guarantees on the Bering.

That reminds me of a friend named Mongo, who I thought
would never die. He seemed immortal and somehow protected
by fate. He had a reputation for skating death at every turn.
Nothing could kill him. He had survived a head-on crash with
an eighteen-wheeler, lost fingers, broken bones, and finally, when
he had enough of testing fate on land, he tried the sea. He worked
on the stacks without a life jacket or safety line, again with the
feeling that accidents happened to someone else, and he fell off
the stack and was dead in minutes. He could collide with an
eighteen-wheeler but not the Bering Sea. That is why when I am
sitting in the captain's chair I insist that the crewmen on the stack
wear a life jacket and hook themselves to a safety line. Sometimes
they argue that the safety line inhibits their movement. Even
with the line, the work still amounts to a delicate and deadly
dance on a heaving platform. Nothing will ever change that.

Each movement of each deckhand is refined to its essence;
economy of effort translates into stamina, which means the difference on a crab boat between success and failure. The drama is
usually played out to the accompaniment of deafening music

strained through monster speakers stacked in front of the fore-peak bulkhead. Heavy metal music drowns out even the howl of the Bering Sea winds. The music gives the crew its edge. Last year, Slayer, Black Sabbath, Judas Priest, Deep Purple, nu metal, trash metal, and glam metal—they all went down. The sounds jolted the crew and kept them alert. Seal bombs did too, when I would throw them out of the wheelhouse window onto the deck below. Like cherry bombs but louder and waterproof, seal bombs are meant to chase marauding seals away from fish caught in gill nets, but I do not know of anyone who actually uses them for that.

The crew comes aboard to work in a blur of day and night. The routine rarely changes, starting with launching pots, usually at half-mile intervals along routes or "strings" determined by the boat's captain and his instincts for where to find the crabs. A pot is lifted by crane from the stacks at the end of a picking hook and deposited on the deck at a launcher, which is a labor-saving metal platform on the starboard forward rail behind the fore-peak. Neal, standing at his station behind the crewman at the pot block, raises and lowers the launcher with his controls. But before he lets the pot go, Russell and Shea must first dance the pot in line with the launcher and finally onto the launcher itself. A careless crewman can easily get caught in the launcher's jaws, which can cut him in half. The pot is dogged down with metal hooks, also activated by Neal, that slide into place and clamp around the solid steel shafts on the pot to hold the pot on the launcher in heaving seas. Shea then detaches the picking hook from the pot's rope bridle while Russell opens the pot's gate and removes three buoys attached to shots of heavy three-quarter-inch line about 400 feet in coiled length. One shot is slung atop the pot, and one (and sometimes more) is either held by Russell or Shea or laid on the deck.

Meanwhile, Richard, the bait man, slithers into the pot to snap the gutted cod (or salmon) and the box of ground herring to the roof of the pot. Shea closes the gate with rubbers. At a signal from the captain in the wheelhouse, usually the sound of a buzzer on deck, Neal pushes levers that lift the launcher. At the angle of repose, the pot slides into the water followed in quick succession by the remaining shots of line and buoys. The boat continues to drive at a steady speed. A half mile later, the picking hook is swung over to another pot on the stacks, attached to its bridle, and another pot is swung to the launcher, and so on.

The pots soak up to forty-eight hours on the sea bottom. Common wisdom holds that the longer a pot soaks, the more crabs will crawl in after the bait. When the boat returns to retrieve the string, the crews work in reverse.

Shea stands ready on the forward starboard rail as the boat approaches a pot's buoys. He throws a grappling hook attached to a thin line, and then reels the line in with the shot line that is itself attached to the pot on the sea bottom. He threads the end of the shot line around the top of the pot block, a circular steel hydraulic winch designed to rapidly raise the heavy pot; the buoys, once they are removed from the water, are thrown out of the way on the deck and the end of the line is placed in a Marco rope self-coiling machine, shaped like a barrel. When the pot reaches the surface the block is halted momentarily while Russell attaches a picking hook to the rope bridle. The pot is swung by crane a few feet along the outside of the rail in line with the launcher, and two crewmen dance the pot onto the launcher where Neal dogs it down. The picking hook is secured. Shea or Russell rolls the stainless steel sorting table from the center of the deck under the pot's gate, which is then opened and crabs pour out with a helpful shake of the dogged-down launcher. Richard removes what remains of the bait. If the pot is not to be returned to the sea, Richard or Shea place the coiled shots and buoys inside the pot. They close and tie down the gate and attach the picking hook to the bridle. Neal swings the pot across the deck to the stacks.

Meanwhile, once the crew has attended to the pot, they sort the crabs. They set females and juveniles aside, measuring their carapaces with hand-held plastic gauges to ensure their legality. State law allows us to keep red king crabs six and a half inches or greater and opilio/snow crab of four inches or greater and tanner/baradai of five and a half inches or greater. Alaska Fish & Game, along with the state police, fines boats that return with more than 1 percent of their catch under the legal size. And the fines amount to $2,500 and $25,000 for the boat. The crew measures with justifiable care, and usually when Russell joins the crew he takes responsibility for ensuring the legality of the catch. Why all these regulations? Simply to make certain—or as certain as anyone can be—that fishermen like me will be catching Alaskan crabs fifty years from now.

As they measure the crabs, either with the eye or the plastic gauge, the crew skids the keeper crabs along a ramp to a stainless steel funnel above the holds. The crew throws the rejected crabs—females or those too small—into large plastic bins called shovel-nosed totes, which the crew eventually empties out an opening at the starboard rail. The crabs sink safely to the sea bottom. The keepers stay in the holds of seawater where bin boards prevent them from being crushed under the weight of their collective mass; one dead crab, which emits a toxin when it dies, can infect and kill every crab in the hold. The crabs can remain on the boat for around two weeks, but not many days more.

The crew repeats the process until their eyes glaze over and limbs sag from fatigue. Each separate action takes place on a platform with the stability of a roller coaster. At some point soon after they first start working on the deck, the crew catches the rhythm of the sea and the boat. The shuffling step needed for balance on a pitching deck becomes unconscious, and the crew can turn its full attention to what they are doing with their hands. The balancing mechanism in the inner ear adjusts to the motion of the Bering Sea, and man and sea become as one. But back on land, when the sea must separate from the man, the effects are as maddening as they can be bizarre. Men look drunk when they have had nothing to drink. They weave and sway while they are standing still, their bodies and minds telling them that they are still at sea. Sometimes sea legs take days and even weeks before they grow steady again on land.

Everyone in the crew watches out for everyone else. Because of the speed of their work and its dangers, the men form a tight team where five different functions are happening at once. But after seventy-two hours of straight and flat-out work, exhaustion wears them down and even can, in the extreme, break them apart. Someone on deck has to be aware of morale. Neal screams at the crew to keep them alert. Russell misses nothing when he is on deck. Through three days of sleeplessness, no one escapes the degrading of senses and alertness. In those final hours, accidents happen and deaths occur without warning.

It is as if crab fishing in the winter on the Bering Sea were combat without the bullets but with all the tensions and mortal fears intact. As with a military unit, at any moment, a crewman may be called on to save a life, and if he is distracted or his senses are dulled by exhaustion, he will not be in a position to save his own life, much less that of anyone else. An attitude of "every man for himself" does not work on a crab boat where shit can happen quickly. In a crisis, with the training of a rifle fire team in a fight, a crewman can find himself in serious danger if his mind wanders. I tell my crews to wipe their minds of girlfriends, debts, or what they will spend their money on—wipe *everything* away but the job. Each crewman must hold up his end of the bargain each minute. Otherwise, another deckhand must cover for him. And that forms resentments, which can be dangerous. Bottom line: A teammate can kill you. You have to trust that he will save you instead.

Off the deck, one essential dominates life at sea: lack of sleep. No clocks tick on a crabbing boat. Last year Shea remarked, "There is no such thing as time out here—no hours, and only days. You work until you go home. Sometimes it is light outside. That's the only difference." Sleep takes over when and where waking stops. There is no middle ground between sleep and wakefulness, no slow settling into the soft arms of Morpheus. Heads will rest on arms on the galley table. Crew will sleep sitting up, and sometimes, for brief seconds, standing up, in daylight or starlight, in bright electric light, in the forepeak on spare rope lines and buoys, in the sauna, or the galley—indeed, any place at all. In the extremes of exhaustion, sections of the brain simply drift into sleep, leaving the rest of the thinking process on its own; in moments that can stretch into hours, the crew loses its ability to shape thoughts into words. They become blithering hulks with blank faces and strangely addled eyes. They begin to hallucinate sleep. These are the moments of maximum danger to themselves and fellow crewmen, and unless the deck foreman gets them off the deck, bad things can happen. The trick is to maintain a balance between alertness and a groggy, stumbling, incoherent state. The mark of a great deck crew is the ability to continue working on this brutal edge.

Last year on the *Time Bandit,* the staterooms, which are fitted with two single bunks each on the main deck and two double beds in the captain's quarters a half level down from the wheelhouse, had a frat house ambience: dirty pants and sweaty

T-shirts, filthy underwear and socks that smell like fish strewn on the thinly carpeted floor, a dank, musty smell of rancid mushrooms, CDs and portable players set up on milk crates, sleeping bags and blankets rumpled on the beds, paperback books and magazines opened here and there. A crab boat is a neat freak's worst nightmare. Out in the galley, ashtrays overflowed with butts, girly magazines were left open, and candy and snack food wrappers built up in a layer of trash. Strewn on the galley's counter were mixings like CoffeeMate in different flavors for the drip coffeemaker, jars of peanut butter and jams, and bread wrapped in plastic bags. (But the boat comes into port spotless after the whole crew turns-to, scrubbing and vacuuming, polishing and buffing, as if they were their mothers on cleaning day.)

Next in popularity to the refrigerator and freezer (with their gallon buckets of ice cream) a wide-screen TV monitor plays DVDs night and day, often without anyone watching. The monitor rests on a built-in dresser bolted to the floor across from the crew's table. The dresser's top drawer contains at least a hundred DVDs. Most feature action and techno-violence, although not all. Last year, Russell was debating whether to watch Reese Witherspoon's *Just Like Heaven*. He mentioned the title to Richard, who was taking a break. Their conversation went like this:

Russell: "You seen it?"

Richard: "Once."

Russell: "Does she show her tits?"

Richard: "Naw. But she almost does."

Russell: "She doesn't do that?"

Richard: "Naw. But it's good anyway."

Off the deck last year, the conversations revolved around sea tales, jokes, food, money, gear, and women. Shea lamented his loneliness and yearning for his girlfriend. He was describing how before he departed, leaving her for the first time since they met, she told him she would not be lonely without him. She had a dildo, the mention of which made him blanch.

Russell asked Shea, "What kind?"

Shea looked down at his hands: "She calls it her 'Pink Elephant.' Shit, that's not something a guy wants to hear before he goes out on a trip. It's gotta have an effect on you, as a guy."

Russell: "And what were you expecting her to get, a one-inch dildo?"

"No, but . . ."

"It's like us with our toys. We want a big-assed Harley, not a little scooter."

Shea was ruminating. "Still . . . 'Pink Elephant.' It's weird."

Russell: "No. What's weird, Shea, is that you sound like you are jealous of an inanimate object."

The chatter can drift to any subject, and usually does. Richard was already planning a vacation to a warmer climate the minute the opilio season closed in March; he was considering Hawaii or Mexico.

I advised him to stay away from Mexico. He asked me why. I told him I have visited Mexico five times. I was thrown into jail three. The first time I got into a fight with a Mexican karate expert. I did not fight back so it was not much of a fight, but I was sent to jail anyway. Another time, someone stole my wallet from me, and when I complained the police put me in jail because I had no ID to show them. The last time I do not know what I did. I told Richard how I could write him a position paper on how to get out of Mexican jails. You need to convince them you have no money, or they will keep you there until hell freezes over, or you convince them you are poor. If they think you come from a rich family, they will go for the family's money. They do not care where the money comes from. Like they asked me, "Do you live in a house?" I told them, "No, I live in a trailer."

The last time I was in jail in Mexico, I stayed long enough to convince them I had no money. They had thrown me in with thirty filthy Mexicans and a couple of stupid gringos. One old guy told me that he had put his money for safe keeping—five grand in cash—in a locker at the airport. The stupid bastard had no idea that some Mexican rifles those lockers each day. He wept when I told him. When they let me out, I went home with nothing except the clothes on my back. Jails are rough and corrupt in Mexico, I told Richard. In the end, for a Bering Sea crab fisherman, jail, no matter where it is, sucks.

After two days of pulling an average of eight king crabs a pot, we were getting frustrated. The fishing for us was as bad as it has ever been. Nothing explained it but bad luck. The other boats were reporting crab (*Northwestern* was pulling eighty crab averages in their pots), and we were lagging well behind the fleet. One pot came up with nothing. Andy said, "There must be a hole in it."

We had our IFQs, which meant we were fishing with 100 pots for a total of 133,000 pounds of king crab. I had no doubt about meeting the quota, eventually, but starting out like this was making me wonder where the crabs had gone. My confidence was slowly leaving me. Hard work with nothing to show grinds on a fisherman's soul. As Andy said, working the deck, "We have to launch the pots anyway, and we have to pull the pots whether there is one crab or 100 in them; the effort is the same." It was clear to me that the crew wanted to fish somewhere else.

Russell added injury to insult. He slammed his funny bone

hard against the steel block. For a minute, he was thrown into a paroxysm of real pain, like he had a football "stinger." He had no idea what had hit him. Watching from the wheelhouse, I saw him fall to the deck and roll over screaming. In another minute he reassured himself that the pain came from a pinched nerve and a sprained elbow. Andy taped his arm, and Russell was off the deck for the day. The funny-bone incident created a pause in the routine. I thought about what changes I needed to make.

Andy and I have hunted crabs for twenty years and we know their habits. We know where to look for them if we are not finding them. Male crabs congregate along the creases in sea bottom inclines like narrow gullies or arroyos. They snuggle against the ridges at around 400 feet where the feeding is good. These inclines, when viewed on a bottom sounder, form silhouettes that unmistakably remind us of different objects and people. Andy and I refer to them in terms like Sombrero, Butt Cheeks, Can Opener, Goose, and Magoo, for the one with the profile of the cartoon character Mr. Magoo. I knew from the evidence in our prospecting pots that the males were not yet separating from the females. They were congregating in potholes on the bottom. We had to go up to the undersea hills where the separation would begin, and I told the crew on deck over the loudhailer in a booming—I hoped ominous—voice, "Let's go where no man has gone before." I told Caveman to chain the stacks for safety's sake, and we struck a heading to take us 220 miles north-northeast of Dutch and well above the other boats in the fleet.

Even in the worst of times, I prefer not to follow the herd. The younger captains will trail behind other boats in hopes of picking up pockets of crab left behind, but they are learning the grounds. Andy and I like to think we know where to find crabs based on long experience. First of all, we know what we saw last year. We have kept notes where we brought up the babies, which we call the recruits. We see what we see from the previous year and find the trends. If we cannot locate crabs quickly, they are probably not there, or so we tell ourselves. We wanted the mother lode—full pots until we plugged our holds with crab.

The weather as usual was miserable, with seas around thirty feet and the temperatures well below freezing. In that area of the Bering Sea, the weather seems never to know what it wants to do. In one thirty-minute period, snow blowing sideways can turn to sleet that forms sheets of ice on the deck and rigging. And then it will stop. It was one of those days to be indoors and snug.

Once we reached the new—and we hoped, unexplored—grounds we set a prospecting string, which we allowed to soak while Neal and I filled a thirty-gallon plastic trash bag with five pounds of flour, tied it off, and out on the deck near the block, attached the bag to the shot line and sent it down with a pot. We used to fill bags like that with shit so that anybody pulling our pots illegally would get shitbagged, but those times have changed. Nobody raids pots anymore.

Once we were picking up the pots, Caveman was working the block for Russell, whose elbow was still hurting, and Caveman was not keeping pace with the boat. He was expending too much energy; he had not yet learned to streamline his movements, and he was getting tired. We rubbed our hands together as he hooked a buoy and pulled in the shot line. He was standing next to the block as Neal, on the hydros, winched up the pot. When the trash bag hit the block, it exploded like a bomb, spraying flour over Caveman, who leaped backward. His face was white and everyone laughed at his surprise. We were still smiling a short time later when our humor turned to alarm.

We were retrieving the last of our pots, moving from one to the next in the string, when another boat, a 130-foot crab scow named *Trail Blazer* appeared on our starboard about half a mile out. We were moving in opposite directions roughly on parallel tracks. When we came abreast we were about 400 yards off. In the wheelhouse, I noticed that the barometer was dropping. We were in for a hard blow. I looked out the windows with my binoculars and fixed on a crewman on the *Trail Blazer*. He was clambering on the pots chaining the stack in anticipation of rougher weather. He was walking on the pot webbing and bars six widths of pots off the deck. It was dangerous to be on the stack in those seas, and the captain of the *Trail Blazer* unaccountably had allowed the boat to drift into the trough. A port-to-starboard wallow threw the boat heavily from side to side.

Andy came into the wheelhouse carrying his video camera. He had mentioned earlier that he wanted to experiment with the new camera. He said he was freezing on deck; he was wearing only rain pants, a sweatshirt and boots. I pointed to the *Trail Blazer*. With only a glance he sized up the danger. He said to me that the crewman had better watch out. The seas were rough; he could be swiped by a wave and disappear overboard and nobody would see what happened. We watched him with our naked eyes; he was now hanging over the side of a six-high stack trying to attach a chain. The captain of *Trail Blazer* was unaware of what his crewman was doing. The scow remained in the trough.

Andy went out the wheelhouse door behind the captain's chair with the video camera. The *Trail Blazer* wallowed with each wave, which swung the crewman, who seemed unaware of the danger he was in, nearly into the freezing water. I looked over again, thinking, *This is fucked*.

Usually when a captain orders a crewman over the side like that, he will jog into the waves and cut his speed. I was about to warn their skipper on the radio of what was happening from our point of view. Andy came back inside the wheelhouse and said,

"God, my hands are cold." I told him I was going to call the *Trail Blazer's* skipper, and I asked him, looking out the window again, "*Where'd that guy go?*"

Andy said, "I just saw him on the stack." But the man I had seen turned out to be another crewman running to tell the skipper.

Seconds later, the captain was screaming on the radio, "*Time Bandit*, man overboard! Man overboard!"

I swung the binoculars. The man was now in the frozen sea two boat-lengths behind *Trail Blazer*. He was blowing air into a malfunctioning life vest. Just as before, when the F/V *Troika's* captain died on *Time Bandit* to my everlasting shame, my legs started to shake with dread. I was not going to stand off this time and watch while another boat fumbled a rescue; the *Trail Blazer* was making a 180-degree turn but the man in the water would have succumbed by the time they reached him. I could angle *Time Bandit* directly without turning and reach the man in minutes. It was go time. I forwarded the throttles to maximum rpms. We could save this guy. I *knew* we could.

I thought of the water temperature—38 degrees—and the condition of the man, who was virtually defenseless in that sea. Seagulls hovered over his head probably imagining him as garbage. I watched the *Trail Blazer* turn, but her crew was not yet deploying a life sling from the crane and no crewman was on deck in a survival suit.

I flipped the switch to activate the general alarm. A siren screamed through the boat alerting the crew, who knew about the emergency without my telling them. Russell was dumping a survival suit out of a bag onto the wheelhouse floor. I do not think I ever saw him move faster. I steered the *Time Bandit* to bring our starboard alongside the man overboard. Down on the deck in the bow Neal was maneuvering the crane in position for a rescue. I thought of the brass key around my neck. For a year after the *Troika* tragedy, I wasn't locking that door again. We were ready to save this man's ass. My feelings were incredibly intense. Right or wrong, I felt that this man had only a few more seconds to live, and *Time Bandit* was all that stood between him and oblivion.

I was hard pressed to figure out his condition. He was not moving. He was not flailing his arms or swimming. Either he was trying to conserve his energy, and thus whatever heat remained in his body, or he had passed out and was close to dying in the water. It was a challenge for me to track him in the waves. He seemed impossibly small from where I sat. One second I would see his head; the next, he was gone. I felt such pity for him. He was a mere pinprick alone on a vast sea.

I brought the bow up beside him and reversed the engines. I swung *Time Bandit* like it was a skiff. Neal was standing on the starboard rail with a life ring in his hands. The man overboard was bobbing in the swells right off the block when Neal threw the ring. The ring landed beyond the man's reach. I jogged the boat to keep him close to our starboard side. Neal threw the ring again.

The man was pleading, "Don't let me die! Please don't let me die!"

"You're not going to die. We got you," Andy told him.

I was yelling at nobody in particular, "We got him! We got you, Bud!"

Andy lifted him onboard. Altogether, once we reached him, getting him on the deck had taken fifteen seconds.

On the deck Caveman grabbed him in a full World Wrestling Federation neck lock. The man was crying and snuffling, "My mom thanks you; my grandma thanks you; my girlfriend thanks you. *You saved my life.*" Caveman was as keyed up as everyone else. We had saved him from drowning. That was true. But he was not yet saved from hypothermia.

Caveman dragged him across the deck and inside the deck door to the cabin. We put him on the floor where the captain had died, and Richard helped him strip off his wet clothes. He wrapped a blanket around him and asked him if he could stand up. Russell walked him to the galley, where he collapsed on the settee. Andy asked whether one of the crew should snuggle naked with him in a sleeping bag to warm him up. The crew looked at one another. Russell started laughing. "I guess he's going to die," he joked.

The man looked at me. "My God, was that scary."

"You're alive, man," I told him.

"I just lost it. It was cold and I just . . . Icy. Caught the chain and . . ."

"You disappeared, man," I told him. "You disappeared." I hugged him, and he was crying with relief. I was too.

I told him, "My legs are shaking. Take your time. . . ."

"Unbelievable," Russell said.

"I wasn't going to let you go," said Andy.

I was puffing hard with adrenaline. "Last time that happened we pulled a dead guy out of the water."

Andy said, "Not this time, huh, John?"

"No, this time we got him."

We waited for his body to react to the warmth. His name was Josh White. He had four minutes to shiver, we estimated, or the indication would be that his core temperature had fallen too low and he would die. He was weeping. I had to get away from him, and I was bawling as I left the room. I do not know if it was for Josh White, or the captain off the *Troika*, or maybe for myself, because the curse was off the boat.

I went up to the wheelhouse. Andy was there. "We redeemed ourselves, brother."

I told the skipper of *Trail Blazer* the news. His attitude struck me as . . . well, different. He wanted Josh White to *swim* back to *Trail Blazer*.

"What was that?" I asked him.

"Put him in a survival suit and tell him to swim back."

I did not get it. Josh White was telling us that today was his thirty-first birthday. What a gift: fall overboard, get rescued, and swim back? I did not think so, and I told his captain my thoughts.

"Well, tell him to take the rest of the day off and celebrate," he said.

Andy and I gave each other looks of incomprehension. What was this guy thinking?

We kept Josh onboard *Time Bandit* and dropped him off the next day in St. Paul in the Pribilof Islands from which he could catch a flight to Anchorage. And feeling huge rushes of endorphin, we set out to return to where we had put down our prospecting pots. And almost like night and day, the pots started to show us money. They came up bulging with king crabs, first with sixty-nine in a pot, then seventy-one. I was doing the "crab jig" in the wheelhouse when Russell indicated with his fingers from the deck that the next pot contained 100, and the one after, 106! The crabs had moved north. We had landed on top of their main mass.

I told Andy, "Nobody will believe us. I'm the Comeback Kid."

The next pot showed 151. We were averaging more than 100 per pot. This was historic.

We dropped another set. Andy put on his cowboy hat for luck. I told him, "I'd rather be lucky than good any day. I found the mother lode."

The string produced numbers I had not seen before: 106,

134—that was when Andy put on his hat—126, 132, 118. It was like dredging up a treasure chest every ten minutes. Red gold!

And, finally, with no place to put more crabs, we headed back to Dutch.

We pulled $320,000 of crabs in thirty-six hours, for a total of 133,000 pounds. The red crabs for the season grossed the boat $500,000. Two-thirds went to the captains and the boat, and a third went to the crew, which meant six percent or $32,000 for each deckhand, less his share, again six percent, of the food and fuel. Not bad for a couple weeks' work.

We met up at Latitudes, where I took possession of the $900 prize for the most crabs per pot. All that cash felt good in my hands; I rang the bell for drinks all around and donated most of what remained to the Fishermen Memorial Fund. Even though it was early in the day to be drinking, Russell shouted over the raised voices, "It's 7:30 in Japan. Let's get drunk."

I will always wonder if our good luck had anything to do with getting the bad luck off the boat. Could the size of our king crab catch really have had anything to do with saving the life of Josh White?

Do Flowers Hurt
When You Pick 'Em?

Andy

Still nothing from Russell. I carry my cell phone in my shirt pocket, even now and then needlessly checking on the volume control, distrusting the instrument because it does not ring. I'm sitting on Rio's back, and Rio is up to his belly in water in the middle of the pond, where the biting horse flies only reluctantly will go. To anyone passing by, we would look strange, a man and a horse in a pond, hardly moving except for Rio's swishing tail. I am finding myself stuck where I am, not knowing about Johnathan.

He has the softest heart of any of us Hillstrand boys. People who do not know him might doubt this; he comes across bold and brash, I suppose as a defensive measure, a sign of fundamental shyness, perhaps? Our mother thought he would grow up to be a veterinarian; he carried insects and small animals in his pockets. He held bees in his hand. He raised and sold teddy bear hampsters to the pet store. When our cat was giving birth to a litter of kittens, she came for Johnathan. He left her to tell us about the babies, and she came back to get him. When we were little kids on the Spit, visitors would leave starfish and other sea creatures on the beach, and John put them back in the water. One time, he asked Mom, "Do flowers hurt when you pick 'em?"

But, notwithstanding any of that, sometimes he can piss me off like nobody else on earth. Before king crab season, he swans into Dutch on a PennAir flight from Anchorage, instead of riding out the rough seas on the *Time Bandit* from Homer; and he arrives like Hollywood with local girlfriends and his buddies all waiting to greet him at the airport. He is the *Time Bandit*'s captain in the king crab season. He knows I will cover for him. That's what I do. But that makes me angrier still. He is a force of nature that I cannot change. And by now, I would not even try.

I do not know where the fishing and our ages and the ownership of the *Time Bandit* will lead us brothers. We could sell out our IFQs and the *Time Bandit* and walk away with a million dollars each. Our boat is a partnership, and if I can build up the horse business in Indiana, I will never have partners again. Selling the boat would get me out of this endless cycle. I wonder how we have stuck with the repetition of seasons this long: From January 15 to March 31 we fish opilio and sometimes baradai like we are now. Then we run *Time Bandit* home, take the crab gear off, and put gear on for herring tendering. We go to Sitka and deliver to Prince Rupert Sound, Canada, through April. We then go back to Homer and prepare for the herring fishery for two weeks, and once that is complete, the boat goes home again. Now, salmon tendering lasts from June 15 in Bristol Bay for forty days, until the end of August, then in Kodiak until late September. And before king crab begins on October 15 we have to tear down the boat, paint the hull, and attend to the gear. The boat never stops—and that is the real meaning of *Time Bandit*.

Are we going to continue as we are now? I just do not know.

Johnathan will want to go on, and Neal will go along with him. I may have to keep fishing, but with my head instead of my heart. But what about the long-term future?

Fishing the Bering Sea was a family affair starting with our dad, but I do not see that in the Hillstrand family's future. My daughters are not interested; Chelsey loves the sea but a career as a fishing boat captain is not going to happen. Neal's two teenaged boys are not going to fish either. Johnathan's son, Scott, may continue but he faces a dilemma of how to live off fishing if he does not own a boat. He will be relegated to life as a deckhand. Earning six percent of the catch might work while he is young, but after a certain age, the work gets harder. His wife Ashley faces a dilemma, as well, as a mother, wife, and woman. Her husband will be off the boat or on the boat. There can be no middle ground. He is either a seafarer or a family man. He has to marry the boat. It is the same choice I made as a younger man. Scott is our last family hope on the sea and it is not looking good.

Fishing as a lifestyle does not get passed down anymore. I do not need to wonder why.

It used to be all or nothing. It was a gold rush. The risks were exhilarating. If we did not pull it off, we lost the boat. Our backs were constantly against a wall. We lived for pressure, the rush, and the adrenaline. But what young person wants that? My brothers and I have fished from the age of twelve. It was ingrained early on in our character. We had the ethic for stress-related work. We were mentally tough. Our dad, mean as he was, gave us this character. We worked hard. He yelled at us, "Pull on the goddamned line, you stupid sonofabitch!" I was pulling 250 fathoms of purse line and every muscle in my body was popping. If I let up for a second, he would yell at me again. That does not happen anymore. Those times are gone.

My brothers and I grew up with nothing. We knew what

hunger was like. Today, parents give their kids everything. Parents know that they are not building their children's character but are helpless to do anything else. Few young people know hunger and real want. They have not experienced what it is like to have nothing. And just something small like a hard life at sea with little to show for the work will not satisfy them. This is America as it is today. And America today is no training ground for Bering Sea fishermen.

The Bering Sea crab industry is moving in a direction that eliminates even the romance of the sea. With rationalization, the industry is consolidating and shrinking. Some 300 boats in the king crab fleet not long ago crowded Dutch Harbor during Derby Days; now 80 boats are registered and about 65 boats actually cast off and go fishing. The canneries are taking over the business from ocean floor to retail shop floor. The deck crews of the future will be hourly workers. The captains will earn salaries. We are dinosaurs.

I Was Tango Uniform

Johnathan

Last December, after king crab season ended, *Time Bandit*'s crew and Andy and I took a short break over Christmas. My girlfriend at the time flew down from Homer to be with me. One evening we rode my Harley to a local bar. We were minding our own business, enjoying a few drinks, when three guys I did not know parked themselves beside us at the bar and started hitting on her like I was not there. She brushed them off politely but she made it clear that she wanted them to leave her alone. I let her handle it.

These guys left the bar and came back more stoned or drunk than before. They would not leave her alone. She is beautiful, admittedly, but this went way beyond that sort of attraction. They were looking for a fight. With a few out-of-bounds remarks from them, she went quickly from uncomfortable to angry. The situation was heating up fast. They started to pump up their aggression. My girlfriend gets hit on often. Most guys get the message and move on. These guys were not taking no for an answer.

I do not get mad easily. But when I do, I can fight to the death.

I am focused and I can smite an army with the jawbone of an ass, as Ezekiel said, I think.

It came to that. I took one guy down on the floor and held my fist in his face. I said, "I don't want it to be this way." He said okay.

I turned around and he got off the floor and punched me from behind. The whole bar began fighting. I tried to stay out of it. The three guys who had bothered my girlfriend went outside. We turned back to face the bar. They came back in and a big sonofabitch grabbed her hair and slammed her forehead against the bar and said he would find her, rape her, and kill her.

I told him, "It's time for you to leave."

The bartender was on the phone to the police when I was taking these guys outside. The fight was quick. I threw the would-be rapist/killer down on the ground and pulled his head back and kicked as hard as I could. Blood flew everywhere. He went limp. His two friends jumped me and hammered away; I have a head as hard as a helmet; you can pound the shit out of me for hours and you will not knock me out. I was wearing them out, and in a real fight that does not take long. My girlfriend screamed and scratched and punched. She fought like a wildcat. She bought me a few seconds to run over and slam-kick the big sonofabitch in the face with my boot. The only thing that moved on him was the blood from his ears.

The police arrived and handcuffed my girlfriend and me. As it turned out, I had kicked the rapist dude into a coma, but the coma could not have been that bad; it gave his brain a rest. He was out of the hospital in three days. I was held in jail over Christmas and New Year's. At the arraignment a woman judge told me that I was looking at 92 months to 120 months. I counted twice to make certain and said, "TEN YEARS!! For a guy defending himself?"

I was Tango Uniform—Tits Up, in other words, Fucked.

I just hate being in jail. It is my greatest fear.

I worried that Mom would find out what happened. I felt bad for her. She came down from Oregon to visit me, and I felt ashamed. She said she loved me, and there was nothing I could ever do that would make her love me less, and that made me feel worse. Once the district attorney reviewed the evidence and testimonies and checked up on the men I had fought, he dropped all charges against me. I was free to go. It seemed that my so-called victims had outstanding felony warrants. Who had started the fight was never in doubt. Still, it was the worst trouble I was ever in.

I do not know what I could have done differently. Maybe I should have left earlier, before the fight got going, but I do not like to be chased out of bars by loudmouth women haters. And I do not go into bars looking for fights. I watch out for some people and avoid them if I can. After all, I am getting older. One thing I can say: I never fought with knives or guns. Not once. If you carry a gun, you are only going to get shot. I learned that when a guy at a party asked me to take him to buy some liquor. We were driving around and he said, "Liquor stores are closed. Stop. Stop over there. I'm going to get some booze."

I said, "What a weirdo."

He smashed the front window and grabbed a case of beer. Back in my car he asked if he could check out a pistol I kept between the seats. While he was robbing the liquor store I had emptied the bullets. I said OK. He stuck it against my ribs. I beat his ass and left him on the highway. I quit carrying guns after that.

This is what I think of now: It is dark.

I can only guess that I have drifted southeast of Augustine Island; I started fishing 45 miles south of the line. It is unlikely that the rip turned me directly south out the Kennedy Entrance and into the Gulf of Alaska; if that had happened I would have encountered—and probably seen lights on—one of the Barren Islands, like Ushagat or the two Amatulis. I could have reason to breathe easier. Those islands can be treacherous without smooth sandy beaches and gentle surf to welcome ashore boats like mine. The downside is the alternative to missing the Entrance. I am moving into, if I am not already in, the entrance to the Shelikof Strait. My course has to be one or the other.

The real point is, I do not know where I am. I have no way to find out. At daylight I might be able to sight a feature that will orient me, but in this darkness, my only hope is for light, or rescue.

On my hands and knees I look for the flare kit, which I think I stored in a locker under the bunk I have been lying on. I pull open the hatch and feel around with my hand until I find a flashlight, which is nearly out of power, with a tenuous dim orange glow at its business end, but the beam allows me to see into the locker. I pull out my Ruger Super Red Hawk, a .44 magnum with bullets in a black Mexican holster and belt. And I find a knife. I open the flare kit. I know better than to hope for a parachute flare. I am not disappointed. These flares—there are three—are simple signal versions consisting of shotgun shells loaded with the flare; they are shot from a plastic pistol frame. They lift up in the air about fifty yards and come down with gravity and burn a bright red for twenty seconds before the sea extinguishes them. If a searcher is looking in my direction and sees that small light, I am rescued; a flare on the sea calls for immediate response from all boats that see it; but if a searcher turns his eyes away for even a second, the flare might as well be invisible. In other words, these signal flares provide a means to reach out to someone on the water but not much of one. I should be more optimistic. The night is black, and a flare is bright; even twenty seconds can be enough. That said, when should I fire the first flare? I look for a light on the water. I see nothing for 360 degrees around the *Fishing Fever*.

On the deck I balance the flare gun in my hand. What comes to mind is the unbelievable profligacy the crew and Andy and I showed last season opilio fishing on the Bering around the Pribilofs. One night—a night as dark as this one now—we were heading back to Dutch with full tanks, in high spirits, and in a rough sea, when Richard mentioned that he had brought on board $1,000 worth of out-of-date flares, in numbers close to 200, some parachute and some signal flares. That gave me an idea. On our plotter I can see where other crab boats were located around us, those passing us, and those moving across our course. The plotter's program identifies the boats by name on the screen, and when I checked the plotter, I saw F/V *Jennifer A*, a crab boat owned by Ian Pitzman, who I grew up with, heading toward us from about three miles out.

We radioed the Coast Guard on Channel 16 that we would be conducting a flare drill.

The crew gathered up armfuls of flares out of Richard's cache. Neal the Eel modified his flares by removing the parachutes and stuffing the tubes with seal bombs. I turned off the deck lights, including our sodiums on the boom. *Jennifer A*, of course, knew our distance and direction relative to them, and who we were. But Pitzman would not be able to see us with his own eyes. We planned to attack with a full salvo at the moment we came abreast of their starboard side. The crew took up battle stations on the rail, like pirates about to take down a king's ship.

I navigated as close as I dared, without making Pitzman uncomfortable, and at the moment we crossed, I yelled on the loudhailer. "It's war!" and the crew let loose a barrage that crossed *Jennifer A*'s decks and lit the night sky an eerie bright red; seal bombs exploded with loud claps and puffs of smoke.

Immediately, Pitzman was shouting bloody murder on the single sideband. What in hell did we think we were doing? We were laughing too hard to reply. Pitzman's crew returned fire, pitifully, we thought, with a couple of signal flares, and by then we had passed each other, and the fight was over. We talked about the attack for the rest of the night.

What I would give for a parachute flare now.

I aim the flare gun at a 45-degree angle and pull the trigger. I feel the recoil in my hand as the flare lifts across the night sky. It creates a pitiful streak and plops into the sea. It burns for a few seconds and goes out. This then is my connection, my communication network, and my outreach to the world. I shake my head and go back inside the wheelhouse.

After the Christmas break last year, I joined the crew back in Dutch to prepare for the opilio season opening on January 15, when the crabs' "in-fill," which means the solid meat in their legs, thickens. The Bering Sea at that time of year is a drama waiting to play out. There is never a script. But the backdrop for everything that happens is made of ice and sleet, freezing temperatures, Arctic ice pack, mean and cutting winds, and high seas.

Opilio season is the crab fisherman's ultimate test. The worst accidents and most harrowing incidents call for heightened vigilance, stoicism, and discipline; in this environment, even small errors can spiral downward into unforeseen and lethal threats. The authorities prepare for the worst: the Coast Guard moves a fourteen-man team with a rescue helicopter to a temporary base on St. Paul Island; the Alaska Wildlife State Police stations its boat, the *Stimson*, a converted 156-foot crabber, in the port at St. Paul, ready to be called out for emergencies.

Before leaving Dutch, our crew, Andy, and I spent a couple of leisurely days resetting the pots with smaller openings and repairing those that had taken a beating in the king crab season. After several years of decline, opies are coming back. With an IFQ of 400,000 pounds, we were confident this season would be safe, short, and happy. We attended the same rituals as before at Latitudes and the Unisea Sports Bar; we ate Chinese food and stocked our cupboards, and we stuffed four tons of herring in the forward reefers. We planned to catch our own cod. An opie can sniff out nothing faster than fresh bleeding cod.

We were contracted to deliver 90 percent of our opies to the 316-foot *Stellar Sea* seafoods processing vessel anchored off St. Paul as a convenience to us and to comply with the rationalization program's goal of distributing the proceeds of crab fishing to varying areas of Alaska. Nearly 142 workers live on the Peter Pan Seafoods vessel and work eighteen hours a day for $7.15 an hour, every day, in what must be one of the worst jobs on the planet.

One hard challenge of the Alaskan fishing industry is to find men and women year after year to work these miserable jobs. Last year, a friend named John "Double Wide" Nordin, a partner in a small—"We shouldn't even be here"—specialty processor called Harbor Crown Seafoods, and one of the nicest and most generous men in the industry, had his Dutch plant humming when, in a lightning raid, INS agents and state police took away most of his key workers, who happened to be illegal immigrants from Guatemala, San Salvador, and the Philippines. These workers kept Harbor Crown's lines moving in freezing temperatures on a hardscrabble island about as far from home as they could go. Nobody was waiting in line for the jobs. The police and INS quarantined them like diseased animals and flew them off the island, leaving Nordin as adrift in his processing of crabs as I am in *Fishing Fever*.

Nordin and his brother James are Americans from Seattle, but they love the country of their family's origin. Each summer, they return to Sweden. Everything Swedish seems not just different but better to them. Alaskan moose were not good enough for brother James. He had to collide with a Swedish one. He told me he was racing down a highway in northern Sweden with a relative behind the wheel of an Audi A6 at 160 km an hour. James was messing with the climate control dial on the dash and looked up in time to see a huge moose trot into the road. He only had time to tell himself, "Aw fuck, I'm dead." He ducked his head; bad things happened. The car T-boned the moose with the loudest explosion he had heard since his time in the U.S. Army. When the car stopped, he and the driver were alive and covered with moose hair and broken glass. The animal was dead in a ditch. The police said Nordin would have been dead, too, if the moose's right front leg had not collided with the column on the driver's side and thrown the animal over, instead of through, the car.

The Nordins are big men. John's hands are the size of a grizzly's paws. He tried fishing when he was younger, but found safety ashore and decided to stay there. He leaves the fishing to the Norwegians, toward whom he shows traditional Swedish disdain. He says, "They like to die."

"But I'm not Norwegian and I fish for crab," I told him.

"Anyone crazy enough to go out on that sea in winter must be Norwegian."

When the INS rounded up his workers last year, Nordin was not flaunting immigration laws. He checks his workers out but does not investigate them. Hiring for his plant in Dutch Harbor, where no labor pool exists to draw from, costs Nordin money that can only be recouped over a full season of labor. Knowingly hiring illegals makes no sense. When he is in Seattle, he scrutinizes potential workers in a typically honest, straightforward manner. He advertises online and in the local newspapers. When recruits show up at his Seattle offices for interviews, he wants to put the fear of God into them by describing his rules—*no* drinking—the weather, and the miserable working conditions on Dutch. He looks at their I.D.s and then swears and yells at them to draw the worst picture of what lies ahead. After a ten-minute break, he calls them back into a conference room. By that time, one in three have cleared out. Nordin says, "I fly them up, house them, give them four meals a day, do their laundry, and then fly them home. I don't want them there, at my expense, only to want to go home before they have done the work they contracted for, at my expense." He pays them premium wages, just as he pays us boat owners more than the larger canneries. In return, he insists on hard work and first-quality fish and crabs. His kindnesses are often repaid; five boats deliver to him and no one else. Some boat captains have pledged to sell to Nordin for less money if the big processors try to run him out of business.

What Nordin seems to have found is a niche where quality trumps price. It makes a certain kind of sense. Every time anyone turns around, fewer boats are catching less of everything: crab, cod, octopi, and pollock. The big processors designed their plants in the Derby days to rush through as many as a half million pounds of fish or crabs a day, but now that capacity is wasted. Nordin arrived in Dutch with a stronger sales department and fish that he swears could have been caught, for their quality, on a hook and line. His company does not have to convince buyers. They need what he is selling.

But that is now. When he started his cannery on Dutch with

his partner Ken Dorris, the conventional wisdom held that he *was* crazy. The big processors, like Unisea and Trident and the Japanese-owned Alyeska and Westward Seafoods, could snuff him out of business. But he is too small for them to bother with. They are the *Bismarck* compared to his *Little Toot*. And John intends to keep a low profile; wisely, he wants to grow in his niche, not compete in theirs.

The state set the quotas for opies last year at 36.6 million pounds and 3 million for their larger cousins, the elusive baradai crab, which are fished in the same season. *Time Bandit*'s quotas were 10,000 for baradai and 250,000 for opies. That, by contrast, was against 92,000 of king crabs we caught in the fall. To catch the opies and baradai, *Time Bandit* was carrying 137 pots, weighing 110,000 pounds, when we set out from Dutch on January 15.

Andy was pumped to get our quotas quickly and get back home. He had shit to shovel. He told me, "Let's bet everything on black—*Time Bandit* black." He was in charge of the boat and the planning. He looked over the results of opie fishing from the previous year. He thought he knew where they could be found. We trusted his judgment, and his enthusiasm was infectious. He planned to take us about 240 miles northwest of Dutch to St. Paul Island and a secret opie ground he knew about just east of the island.

As we were leaving Dutch Harbor, the hulk of the SeaLand, a container carrier that had foundered in murderous Bering Sea waters and had been towed into the harbor, lay like a dead leviathan half on its side in shallow water. Andy sat in the captain's chair with me beside him. I was going along for the ride and to be with my brother. I thought that I might work the deck, but at my age, I am used to the comforts and warmth of the wheelhouse when the sun comes through the windows. I could stay home. But with the sea in my blood I would not miss going out one more time every time.

The one time I did sit out a whole crab season on land—two years ago, because *Time Bandit* was in dry dock for repairs—I felt dead. My soul left me. Sitting in town, knowing Andy and my friends (and the crabs) were out at sea on other boats, I was like a salmon that does not make it up the river. That winter, I missed the fishing like a kid misses Christmas. Each year when that first pot comes up, I *am* like a little boy who cannot sleep with excitement. I feel like Santa gave me my first banana-seat bike when that first pot is full.

We were six hours out of Dutch when the state authorities— I do not recall whether it was Fish & Game or the State Wildlife Police—reported over VHF Channel 16 that our delivery vessel, *Stellar Sea*, had reported a fire in its engine room. A Coast Guard cutter was being called out to assist and investigate.

We were fucked. So was any other boat in the crab fishing fleet that was scheduled to deliver to *Stellar Sea*.

The Coast Guard towed the crippled processor into St. Paul. Heavy damage required a tug to help *Stellar Sea* from St. Paul into Dutch for repairs. That left us with two weeks and nowhere to deliver our opies. If there was a silver lining, our holds were empty when the *Stellar Sea* fire broke out. Andy asked me what I thought. We did not have many options. We did not want to return to Dutch empty, and we could not fish for opies, which left us with baradai. We had a small quota. We had the time. And we could deliver these crabs to any processor we pleased. I told Andy, "It's all good; it's all fishing."

Andy both agreed and disagreed. Recently no one had fished baradai, which were fished nearly to extinction in the Bering twenty years ago until the state stepped in and protected them for a decade. They rebounded, but baradai are a difficult catch. When they were told, the crew grumbled. They had to reset the pots, which was not as difficult as they made it seem. And when Andy looked at his bottom plotter and found a likely prospecting area, the crew launched eighty pots over eighty miles, one every ten minutes.

While the pots soaked Andy fretted over the weather, with a 960-millibar low closing in from the northwest. He predicted thirty-five-foot seas and seventy-knot gusts. He worried how many pots the deck crew could pull before the worst of the storm reached us. Meanwhile, he kept his eyes on the seas and the deck. *Time Bandit* was traveling in the ditch, jogging into the sea, taking the waves head-on. Every now and then a "viper" or "growler"— a whitewater curler on top of a wave that pops the bow with the speed of a striking snake—would hit the bow. To give the crew warning, Andy, who could see clearly over the bow into the oncoming seas, shouted over the loudhailer, "Move! Watch out! Watch out!" And the crew ducked and held on. Andy is particularly sensitive to vipers. He and Neal once were working on deck when a rogue wave with a viper washed over the bow and the starboard rail; six feet of green water poured onto the deck and only luck saved them from being washed overboard.

Hurriedly, the crew pulled the pots to beat the weather. Their initial excitement turned to gloom when they realized, on closer inspection of the full pots, that out of every 400 crabs, only 15 were keepers. The throw-backs were too small, female, or "dirty"—crabs with shells darkened by barnacles. This kind of fishing was not worth the effort, but a crab fisherman does not expect to find a sweet spot the first time every time.

The sea was starting to worry the crew. Their footing on the deck was getting slippery. Each pot that came out was rebaited and sent back down. Work that was fast and demanding pushed them to their limits. At one point, Richard, standing by the launcher, was poised to send the buoys overboard after a pot was launched. A wave slapped the bow and sped down the rail just as the buoy line skittered across the deck and around Richard's ankle. All 750 pounds of the pot plummeted to the bottom. Richard, seeing the immediate danger, had only a couple of seconds to untangle the line; he jumped and danced to free his ankle. He bent over and slapped the buoy, which flew up and wrapped around his other ankle. He was a second or two away from going over and down when the line flew off his legs and slipped over the side with the buoy.

Richard stood in one place, a look of shock on his face. He stared down at his ankles, half expecting to see himself jerked and dragged down. With a nervous laugh, he told Russell, "I got away with one on that."

From the bridge, Andy told the crew, "That got serious real fast. I hope you guys are carrying your knives."

He felt responsible for the poor showing. "This is the worst season so far for me ever," he told me. "Somebody should go to jail for this." He clapped his white cowboy hat on his head and stared out the forward windows. "This is just a huge clusterfuck with fuel money going down the drain." He reached for the loudhailer and called the crew off the deck, deciding to let the remaining sixty pots soak until the storm blew through. Moments after the crew came inside, a thirty- to thirty-five-foot rogue hit the *Time Bandit* over the starboard rail. The boat shuddered. Green water poured over the deck. The powerful wave ripped the 200-pound Marco King coiler off its bolts and laid it on its side. Andy said, "I'll fish through almost anything, but this weather worries me."

Time Bandit jogged into the sea, and everyone held on.

Inside in the galley, Richard, a self-confessed sugar junkie, braced his elbows on both sides of a two-gallon container of ice cream. He was staring into the middle distance. He said, "The hardest part of this job is just keeping my balance. That's what takes it out of you. You have to keep your head about you and feel the movement of the waves. Sometimes you worry if another crewman is doing something stupid, like if by mistake he throws the line around *your* neck, and I'm overboard. Out there just now, I do not know how that happened. It was not a mistake on my part. I know, nobody ever admits to mistakes. But this was not one. It was a real accident that could have been a whole lot worse. Real accidents, not just stupid mistakes, really do happen." And he plunged a spoon into the ice cream.

Andy, in the wheelhouse, was deep in denial. "I find the crab and I fish the crab. It never happens that you just land on them," unless, of course, you just land on them. He started talking about one year that stuck in his mind. "That year I could do no wrong. It was my peak. We never pulled bad pots. We brought in a total of 1.7 million pounds of crabs, in two months and a week, and my guys earned $72,000. I was invincible."

"What about now?" I asked.

"I am vincible. But that year there was ice all over and every other boat in the fleet quit and went in. And that was when I landed on the mother lode." Andy looked out over the deck. He said, "Maybe this weather will move the crabs onto the pots."

To sit out the storm, Andy decided to put into St. Paul Island for groceries, which is to say, for a night on the town. St. Paul Island is a bleak low-lying, barren island of wind and more wind that blows across the Bering Sea from Siberia. We tied up at the dock in front of an abandoned cannery at the bow of the *Stimson*, the Alaskan State Wildlife Police's patrol boat. Small black wild foxes scurried over the snowdrifts hunting for rats at the cannery. The sun was setting. It was colder than cold. The crew,

Andy, and I piled into the island's grocery store looking for fresh bread; we spent more than $1,000. We paused for a drink at the island's only bar, which was unheated. The floors were bare, but liquor bottles filled the shelves. We ordered drinks and settled into conversations with the native Alaskans who hang out there. One was telling jokes to his friends. "Knock, knock, who's there? Dishes. Dishes Who? Dishes your girlfriend from Naknek." We laughed to get along. The local natives keep separate from the fishermen. Some of the crew played pool. On the wall behind the table a sign warned, NO HITTING PEOPLE WITH POOL STICKS OR THROWING BALLS AT ANYONE. The St. Paul Island bar is that kind of place.

We threw back a few more drinks to insulate us on the ride in the back of a pickup truck across the island to a small housing development where federal government employees live; they work for the National Weather Service and National Oceanic and Atmospheric Administration. We were going to dinner at the home of the Rex Morgan family, who had invited us over single sideband radio a day ago. Mrs. Morgan served baked chicken and corn on the cob, which was a break from Neal's cooking, and the crew watched sports on a jumbo screen TV. Outside the wind howled and the black-furred foxes patiently waited in the snow-drifts in the back of the house for scraps. The lives of these dedicated civil servants like Rex are unimaginably hard. Without them, crabbers would be largely ignorant of the local weather patterns and the conditions of the sea.

When we left St. Paul harbor the next morning, the weather stayed bad. Andy ordered the crew out to rig the pots for cod; at least if we were not catching crabs, we could bring up bait, and maybe new, fresh bait would make a difference in what we caught. The cod crowded the pots as the storm blew through. With the fresh bait, the crew set eighty prospecting pots that came up with disappointing numbers. The weather had not pushed the crabs toward us as Andy had hoped. We did not know where to find the baradai. Russell said, "We are catching snails."

We spent the next two and a half days prospecting for baradai. The morale of the crew sank. Nobody wanted to talk about fishing. The crew went to their rooms as soon as they had eaten. A funk settled on the boat under the weight of our collective failure. Responsibility rested with Andy, who was supposed to see crabs 400 feet under our hull, and his supersight was failing him. The crew was working the deck for nothing.

Andy was disappointed in the whole IFQ system under rationalization.

The next eighty pots began to show a difference. After a couple more pots, we knew we were approaching a hot spot. Pots began averaging 200 crabs—huge for baradai. The mood of the crew lightened. The weather cooperated. We thought we could bring up our baradai quota in no time. But at sea, no one counts his crabs too early.

Andy heard the sound of the engine change. He throttled back and on the loudhailer told Neal to come to the wheelhouse. Neal knew right away the meaning of the engine's sound. A wave had pushed a pot line under *Time Bandit*'s hull and the starboard main prop had tangled around the three-quarter-inch line. The shaft seized up as the line tightened. Andy ordered the crew to cut the line from the pot. And a $1,000 plus pot plummeted to the bottom.

"What's going on?" Andy asked Neal.

"We're fucked," he replied.

To disentangle the prop, Andy would have to dive under the hull and check out the damage. And right now, a couple hundred miles from Dutch, he had to make certain that he did not further entangle line in the other prop. We had no choice but to limp back to Dutch on one engine with dicey steering.

Times like these test a fisherman's patience. But on that day they gave us an appreciation, which we do not always admit to, of the new rules of crab rationalization. Under the Derby, this prop snarl might have doomed our opie season, but probably not. Now, with new rules, no one could take our IFQs from us. There was no reason for dismay. Maybe rationalization took away our license to catch a bonanza of crabs, but it gave us a safety net. Right now, we felt disappointment but not despair.

Back in Dutch, with *Time Bandit* tied up at the dock, Andy donned a dry suit, flippers, gloves and hood, a regulator, and a compressed air tank. He dove into the thirty-six-degree water off the dock: a pot line had indeed wrapped around the prop shaft. He cut through the nylon-and-hemp line with a serrated knife. The repair took an hour. A short time later, as we were preparing to cast off, a state police pickup drove on the dock and stopped beside *Time Bandit*. A trooper waved at Andy to come down from the wheelhouse. He wanted to talk.

"What now?" Andy asked me.

I could only shake my head.

What now was Caveman.

I have no idea how or why we hired him. He seemed to have appeared out of nowhere. Andy and I already knew that Caveman, wherever he was from, loved to sleep; he truly never seemed fully awake. For the other men in the crew, getting him out of bed was a regular chore. He never "got" it the same way the others did. And now, the police wanted him on an outstanding warrant for DUI in Alaska. The officer explained that Caveman's name had triggered a hit when he was running crew licenses through a national police database.

I told Andy, "I thought he told us he had postponed his court date."

"I guess he lied."

Caveman was one of Neal's hires. Andy gave Neal an evil look. Caveman's crime was not serious, as crimes go, but the officer cuffed him anyway. He was frisking him spread-eagle against his truck, when I offered him a parting thought. "Don't worry, Caveman. For dinner they have sandwiches and cocks, and they are all out of sandwiches."

Richard said, "Why don't we just leave him in jail?"

We might have, too, if we were not a man short on deck and had to catch up after too much prospecting and too little to show in the holds. Added to that was the delay with the entangled prop. Luck was not giving us a break, and now we had no other choice but to bail Caveman out and bring him back on the boat. We had no time to trawl the bars for another crewman.

That afternoon we paid out $500 with cash from our pockets and an ATM; the whole crew chipped in. The paperwork for Caveman's release was ready when we arrived at the jail. He came through the security doors looking sleepy. What could we say? Nothing would change him. He looked as if the prison experience had exhausted him. The minute after we cast off *Time Bandit*, he was fast asleep.

A Fork in the Road

Russell swore he saw a flare. Its distinctive red light was so fleeting and tiny against the sky it could have been a trick of his eye, or something *in* his eye. But it was something, where for hours there had been nothing. He jumped on the radio to call Johnathan's boat. There was no reply. He stared in the flare's direction for fifteen minutes through the binos. If it was a flare, it came at a moment when he had nearly reached a fork in the road. The Kennedy Entrance lay to his left, the Barren Islands were off his port bow, and the entrance to the Shelikof Strait was off his starboard bow. He had to choose which direction to take. The flare, if that was what it was, came from the right, and without further hesitation he headed there.

In time he passed Augustine Island. Ahead looming in the dark was the protrusion of Cape Douglas at the northeastern end of the Strait, which poses a constant danger to boats traveling between Anchorage and Cold Bay, out the Aleutian chain and beyond. There are no lights and radar reflectors to mark the cape, but Johnathan might not have been in a position to benefit from those aids anyway if he had discharged the signal flare.

Russell could only estimate the distance and time to Cape Douglas. He was less than trusting of Dino's *Livers End*. Since he did not know its traits, its strengths and weaknesses, he wanted to take her easy. The engine sounded strong and steady. The generators worked fine. The boat was lit up like a lighthouse. He was making progress, he hoped in a direction that would end with *Fishing Fever* in his sights by full morning light.

I Had Better Get It Together

Johnathan

The tiniest hint of the pre-glow dawn shows in the east behind the peaks of towering mountains along the coast. Darkness is all around *Fishing Fever*, but the promise of light lifts my mood. I shake out one of two remaining Winstons, fire it up, and suck down its delicious, calming smoke. I restrict myself to two inhales and pinch off the ember with my thumb and forefinger. I slide the butt into my pocket for later.

Fishing Fever tells me what she is feeling. She reacts to the water sloshing at her hull; she sends me indications of changes in rips and currents and tides. She seems in the grip of competing forces. There is the height of the sea, which has not increased through the night but remains around fifteen to sixteen feet. This causes me discomfort. The boat rocks in the troughs. The wave frequency has changed; the boat sways like a toy in a washing machine on wash cycle. The currents are strong here and move against the tide. This body of water is fighting itself and anyone riding on it.

I remember the time I was captaining the *Debra D*, out of Mount Vernon, Washington, during opie season in mid-January on the Bering Sea. The boat was carrying 24,000 pounds of frozen bait cod in boxes on the forward deck. We were jogging into heavy seas when we took a huge wave over the bow rail that knocked the entire boat sideways, and the bait broke loose of its chains and slid across the deck to the launcher. In less than ten seconds, we were in those seas with a 40-degree list to starboard; we were going over. The crane controls were underwater. I started jerking out our survival suits, and we waited and watched; the crew ran down to the deck. By some miracle, the boat stabilized itself long enough to allow the crew to shift the eight tons of bait back into the center of the boat. That was as close as I ever have come to sinking aboard anything but smaller boats and skiffs when I was a kid.

I am hungry now but have no intention of eating another raw salmon. In the last hour, my hand touched the bottle of Crown Royal, which remains sealed. There will be time to quench that thirst when I am out of this *stupid* mess, one of those incredible incidents that happens to other people. My stomach growls, probably from the Winston, and in the wheelhouse I twist open a bottle of water, which soothes my stomach and makes me feel like smoking the remainder of the butt.

We launched again from Dutch last year with a clear prop and a court date for Caveman. We pointed our bow in the direction of the Pribilofs. With our quotas intact and a different processor ship on station, we approached St. Paul Island in fair but extremely cold weather and began to pick up the pots we had left on the seafloor when the prop snared the line.

The soak proved helpful. We went from snails when we last

pulled pots in this string to 500 a pot now. The storm had moved the crabs onto our gear. Finally, we were finding good fishing. The crew was feeling good enough to joke with Caveman. He clearly resented what he perceived as their lack of respect. It seemed obvious to me that he had not earned points when he told me that he had cleared up the matter of his court date. He was getting on my nerves.

After the storm, the sea calmed. But the calm I detected around St. Paul was different, by which I mean unique. These seas were small with high winds and extreme cold. That signaled that the Arctic ice pack was moving south.

Two types of ice haunt the Bering Sea. One is called fast, which is another term for ice that holds fast to a point of land. Fast ice can spread a few yards to hundreds of miles depending on the depth of the water, the air and water temperatures, and the winds. Usually, fast ice does not threaten mariners. It gives a home to polar bears, walrus, and seals.

Its cousin, pack ice, presents a grave danger to men at sea. This ice is not anchored to land but drifts with the wind and currents on the Bering southeast from the Siberian coast. The extreme weight and thickness of pack ice dampens the sea swells and with a less agitated motion of the water, the sea turns more rapidly to larger and thicker fields of pack ice. The sea breaks up the solid ice to create ponds of open water called *polynyas* and long, linear, open cracks called leads, which form a maze of navigable water for boats trapped in pack ice. But the thickness of the ice can tear open the thin three-eighth-inch metal hulls of fishing vessels like *Time Bandit*. A one-two punch hits when pack ice slowly pushes a boat toward fast ice or simply toward the shore with no means of escape. This rarely happens, but every captain on the Bering Sea in February and March worries about the peril.

This happened to the F/V *Alaskan Monarch* in the winter of 1991 when she lost steering and was caught up near St. Paul. The Coast Guard was called out to rescue her, but by the time a helicopter arrived the pack ice had already pushed *Monarch* onto the heaps of jagged rocks leading to St. Paul harbor. The helicopter crew rescued four of the *Monarch*'s six crewmen off the deck but two others were swept into the sea by a wave backing off the shore. The helicopter quickly plucked them to safety. Ever since, the twisted, rusting, and torn bow section of the *Alaskan Monarch* on the rocky shore has served as a grim warning to any boat that enters St. Paul harbor.

By reading the signs of the wind blowing from the southeast at thirty-five knots and the seas an eerie calm, it was clear to me that the pack ice and the *Time Bandit* were on a collision course— off St. Paul Island. Usually by April, the pack's southernmost fringe, which angles across the sea from northwest to southeast, slicing our opie grounds in half, extends as far south as the Pribilofs. I know how to maneuver a boat in ice but what worried me was that the processor had anchored the *Stellar Sea*'s 360-foot replacement, *Independence*, close to the shore, indeed, close enough to trap a boat in the pack.

We needed to meet our delivery date and time, or else the processor would send *Time Bandit* to the back of the line. And that meant the added worry that the opies in our tanks would not survive. That would count as a loss to the boat of more than $200,000.

This seemed screwy. We were about to push into the ice pack to reach the *Independence* with the hope that we could deliver the crabs to the floating processor and get out again before the ice trapped us.

But a 113-foot boat is a challenge to navigate in icy alleyways. With Andy gone—he had abruptly left the boat in Dutch to fly home to Indiana; Sabrina had asked him as a special favor to come home to attend the wedding of her nephew, and of course he agreed—I was alone in the wheelhouse, and there was never a time in our lives when I needed his calm and confidence more than I did now.

During most of the fishing year, I take the *Time Bandit* for granted. She is seaworthy and trustworthy. She can go anywhere safely. I can operate and maneuver her with the certainty and finesse of twenty-seven years' experience. Her quirks are second nature to me. Her sinking or foundering would never enter my mind, just as anyone else would never imagine his house burning to the ground. But now, the thought of trapping the boat more than entered my thinking. And if anything happened to her, I would be to blame. Her loss would be equivalent to losing our father. My brothers would understand the events that led up to her loss, but they would have doubts about me forever after, and I would lose part of myself. My confidence would shatter; it would not matter to me one bit that pack ice had wrecked her. *I* had wrecked her. And I would live with that guilt the rest of my life. I have visions of ice sheets around her hull, with nowhere to escape, and the engines straining to move her through ice thirty inches thick, with the bow creasing and the water pressing in. I had better get it together.

We continued to pull pots; we were filling our holds with opie gold. Each pot that contained 1,000-plus opies rang up the cash register at $1,800. Shea looked at one brimming, squirming pot and said, "There's a new pair of skis." Russell wrestled Richard to the deck; they were behaving like happy puppies. "We are finally making big money," Russell said. "This is what I *live* for."

I went down on deck to share in the fun. I told them, "This is a good way to end the season," and the crew renewed its efforts, knowing that we were back on our original schedule. The day continued bright and the ocean's calm made the work easier and faster on deck. Ice from 20-degree ambient temperatures coated the boom and the forepeak and the planking, but the crew was jubilant, knowing they could now return early to Dutch. Neal winched the last pot on the launcher and in another few minutes, Richard flicked his fingers signaling 650 opies. We were ready to deliver. We wanted to go home.

With the crew tucked in bed for the night, I headed for St. Paul Island. About three miles off the island, the ice pack appeared out of the mist. I cut one main engine and crept with one prop at one knot through broken chunks of ice, praying that this would be the worst of the pack until we had offloaded the crabs and headed south. Over VHF I learned that the state had closed the St. Paul harbor, warning that even those protected waters might freeze over in the cold. I did not like the sound of that. According to what the State Wildlife Police reported, the temperature had dropped enough to freeze even the protected salt water in the harbor. I wanted the backup of a place to shelter *Time Bandit*. The harbor was the only safe haven for nearly 280 miles around.

I waited to see what happened. For right now, I was trying to maneuver *Time Bandit* like a 113-foot skiff, around this sheet ice and down small opening leads. When the ice, with some sheets thirty inches thick and weighing 125,000 pounds, came in contact with the bow, *Time Bandit* boomed with a hollow sound like I had pressed my ear to an abyss. I *felt* for the boat. This was not *Time Bandit*'s role. Her hull was not made for this kind of sea, and her rudder and props were too fragile for contact with the thick ice blocks. She would go anywhere at sea that I asked her except here, against this solid water.

Three miles of ice stood between the *Independence* and the

Time Bandit. I could see her boom lights. But those separating miles might have been the circumnavigation of the globe. We had to get through the ice to that processor. Something weird was happening to me. I felt that if I could huddle *Time Bandit* close to the processor, which was anchored firmly on the bottom and enjoyed the protection of a double hull, *Time Bandit* would be safe from harm. Maybe the old safety-in-numbers bromide had taken over, but seeing the sodium lights on the processor's booms comforted me. Our progress was a slow agony. We moved three miles in five hours; we could have walked the same distance across the ice in less than two hours.

At last we tied up alongside *Independence*'s dark and yet welcoming hull. The day was cold and bright, but the worst seemed behind us. The crew came out on deck and assisted with the offloading. Deck hatches had frozen shut in the night, and Neal and Shea snapped four stout lines trying to free one lid with the crane. But eventually the *Independence*'s crew was able to hoist down the brailers into the hold, and their workers stood on the crabs while pitching them into the canvas-sided containers; each was weighed and tallied as it was lifted out. The brailers signified money—a total that day of $216,551, which was not bad considering at one point only a few days ago I thought I would have to write off the opilio season completely. The crew had money to take back to Dutch; they could add opilio shares to their king money and live until the next season. I felt that I had done my job.

With the last brailer emptied, I braced myself to cast off from *Independence*. But in reality, I had nowhere to go. I could have forced my way into St. Paul Island's harbor, against the advice of the State Wildlife Police, but I did not; for once I chose to follow their advice. That left me with no choice but to run for clear water three or five miles south of *Independence* and hope for the best between here and there.

The crew had no further work to do, and after a day of laboring with the offloading, I told them to take it easy; sleep. Caveman snapped to like a plebe at West Point. The sky was darkening. Night was falling. It was bitter cold. I did not dare to run the boat on two engines in the ice and so, as before, we headed out at an even slower pace—half a knot—than when we entered the pack.

As darkness closed around the *Time Bandit*, the temperature fell. The ice moved south. The slow progress ground us down; each hollow sound of the hull hitting the ice slabs made me wince. Over the span of two hours we moved one mile away from the *Independence*. Mother nature was telling me that I was not going home tonight. In light of this, I laughed, but not a funny laugh; it was a psychotic sound that reflected the sheer insanity of this predicament. We ground to a complete halt in the ice, which was tightening its hold. The breaks simply froze together and disappeared. I could see neither *polynyas* nor leads in the reach of the sodium lights. I had nowhere to move.

The hull boomed against the building ice as it broke leads of a boat length. But huge chunks of jagged ice erupted from the broken solid mass, and these threatened to rip into the hull. I craned my head out the window. The cold was unbelievable. The lights of the *Independence* shone brightly in the distance. I made the decision to leave the southerly track. We were not going to reach open water through ice that was rapidly thickening. The tension was tightening in my chest. I was smoking one cigarette off another. I had considered myself a veteran at handling pressures, but this now reached a new level of intensity.

I made the decision to turn around and return to the *Independence*. Making a 180-degree turn with a 113-foot platform in the middle of slab ice had its challenges. By backing up and laying on the throttles I risked shearing off the rudder or bending a shaft or fracturing the prop. I could feel the resistance in my hands on the throttles. I thought about how I had laughed at Mike Myers as Austin Powers in the movie, turning around a golf cart in a corridor that was only inches wider than the cart was long. With a boat, a similar maneuver was no laughing matter. *Forward, backward, forward, backward,* slowly turning by degrees, until at last the *Time Bandit*'s bow was aimed toward the lights of *Independence.*

We returned to her thrall through ice that had closed and thickened in our wake. Backtracking that single mile was measured in Winstons and coffee. The crew stood near me in the wheelhouse adding their eyes to mine. We were stationary in the water half a mile off the coast. Neal said the winds were shifting out of the south, which could signal that the ice pack would start moving again. The next few hours would tell. I advised the crew to get some sleep until I decided on a new course of action.

Sitting in *Fishing Fever*'s wheelhouse, smoking, I was reminded of how fundamentally I am entwined with nature when I am at sea. At times like these, I really do think these things, these big thoughts that never ripple through my brain on land. Some people might think of this connection to nature as obvious, but not me. Usually I take for granted that nature is my master every minute I am on the sea. I can decide nothing independent of her immediate presence—the wind, weather, seas, temperatures, the fish and crabs. I am their slave. They dictate my fate. I am as a farmer, dependent on weather for his crops, on an unstable, rippling, ever-changing, and perilous land.

Does this make me different from people who live with

buffers between their daily existence and the rawness of nature? Absolutely, yes, it does. It makes me a daily survivalist who is innately wary and in fear of change. I am filled with abandon when I return to land, where I have nothing like the sea to fear. What is to fear on land that can compare to a boat on the Bering Sea? Do I fear that I will be thrown off my Harley or beaten in a bar fight? Is this why I am like I am? Is this the reason Andy wants to spend more of his life working with the quintessential *land* animal? Is this why, his conscious desire notwithstanding, he goes back to the sea year after year, as if sirens were calling him toward jagged rocks on the shore?

I pondered my predicament in that ice pack. I knew what I did wrong. I ignored my cardinal rule. I had wanted, more than even the safety of my boat, to deliver my catch on time to the *Independence*, and thus cash in on $216,000 of crabs in our holds. I had fallen prey to the logic of the new system. If I missed my delivery date, I would go to the back of the line, and my crabs would all die. I had defied my basic instincts as a captain by sending *Time Bandit* through the pack ice. In most of our lives, we get away with our mistakes. Nothing touches us with absolute inflexibility. But that is not nature's way. She demands her payment for any small transgression. And now I was paying dearly for mine.

The ice pack changed again. This seemed like the devil at work. The wind must have shifted in the dark. Through those night hours, the temperature dropped further and the wind swung around from the north. More pack ice joined that which was already pushing around the island. Bay rollers under the ice undulated the flat shiny plane around our hull. I felt these rollers grinding the ice against our hull. The force of the wind on the ice was pushing us toward the shore. The engine sawed when the prop struck broken ice blocks and the sound pierced to my soul. The engine quit twice, and the engine alarms sounded below. I was not going to let nature wreck *Time Bandit* on the land, no matter how few choices remained to me. She would go down, if that was her fate, but she would never die like the *Alaskan Monarch*.

I had to make a desperate run for open water; I had to get away from the shore. I wanted the crew to be ready for any contingency. They had not slept in two and a half days, except for this three-hour nap. I flipped the switch to activate the boat alarm. I shouted over the sirens to the crew deck for them to get up. I needed to share with them our troubles.

Shea, Russell, and Neal were out of bed at once, dressed and ready; Richard followed soon after. They stood by me in the wheelhouse looking out through the sodium lights at the ice floes, offering advice and consolation. I needed Neal and Russell especially to help me decide what to do, how far to go, and what stress to put on the engines. Would the screw take the beating? Or would the ice jam the rudder shaft into the lazarette, flooding the boat? These were immediate possibilities. Should we simply shut down the engines and let the wind and ice determine our fate?

Too long later, Caveman came up the stairs, dressed only in sweatpants and rubbing his eyes. He had heard the alarm, woken up, and then had gone back to sleep.

"What's going on?" he asked at the top of the stairs.

This question made me irrationally angry; I was on edge. I needed sleep. I felt shockingly alone.

"Just shut up or I'll kick your ass," I told him. "We are in trouble."

Caveman stood with his arms folded across his bare chest.

I told him, "We might have to get in survival suits. Wake up, get some clothes on, and get some coffee. We are trying to get out of this ice." I looked at him. I was truly angry with him. I said to Shea, "I don't know what kind of guy goes back to bed when the alarm goes off. But I am looking at one now."

Caveman stood at the top of the stairs, I thought almost defiantly.

"You! Caveman! Get dressed!" I turned to Shea and said, "Thank God there are people onboard who actually care."

I tried to advance the throttle but *Time Bandit* was having none of that now. The boat did not budge. The ice rumbled and boomed against the hull.

"This isn't a pretty sight," I told Richard.

The ice was forming in forty- and fifty-foot jagged chunks.

I sent Neal to the forepeak hatches to check on the bow for leaks.

The computer plotter, in which I had input Dutch as our destination, indicated an Estimated Time of Arrival: "NEVER."

Caveman appeared in the wheelhouse. At least now he was dressed.

"I don't yell for no reason," I told him.

If the boat went down, Caveman would not have been prepared to save himself with no clothes on. A boat can go down in four minutes flat. We were not in immediate danger. But Caveman was not using his head. He was behaving like a caveman. If I had told him, "Go drop that anchor *now*," he would have not had his shirt on. And what if our collective safety required the anchor to be dropped now, not when he was ready? I had a right to be mad. I hate captains who scream at their crews. Screaming accomplishes nothing. This once I felt justified.

But I was also mad at something else about Caveman that was under my skin. He was *always* late.

Caveman remarked, "I know I'm not getting in this cold water," as if he would have a choice.

Neal came back to the wheelhouse to report that ice was bending the steel in the bows. At the moment, the dents were not an immediate threat to the boat. The paint had chipped off the inside of the hull, which the ice had not yet breached. Neal said that he had never heard such sounds before, "like something from another world," he said.

Caveman must have thought over what I told him. He came up to the wheelhouse angry about how I had singled him out. I was not prepared to argue. I had said what I felt. I would not apologize. He punched me once in the nose and once in the ear. I said, "That was pretty good. You better get out of the wheelhouse." He punched me a third time, in the throat. I said, "*That* hurt." I was going to split his nose. Instead, I hit him on the top of the head, once, and knocked him out. I dragged him out of the wheelhouse. When he came to I said, "You can either finish this fight or you can finish this season."

For the next four and a half hours, nerves held us together as captain and crew. If a boat weighing 298 tons can move gingerly, *Time Bandit* did. I maneuvered her like a skiff with the throttles, on and off, steering left and right with the leads in a heading south. The sea swell broke the ice and created a path that was no more than a boat's length. We moved boat length by boat length. The sun came up. I could see clear water ahead. We reached the pack's fringe. In another half hour, we went clear. We had made it through my worst night.

"Dude," I told Richard, "that took a year off my life."

I should ask a lawyer to legally change my initials from J.H. to T.U. I am Tango Uniform like never before. The minute the light intensifies in the east I can see where I am in this universe. The rain lowers the sky down to the sea. A mist is changing to fog. This world is a dull gray. No one will know I am gone. The look of the cliffs in this weather is like the Land Before Time. The sight off my starboard side chills me. Jagged rocks heap along a mountain wall that rises four or five hundred feet to a short plateau of snow and ice that beats down on my face like sharp slivers. I refuse to put on my life jacket. That is not who I am. I know I can get ashore and cling to the rocks. I tie the ropes of my bumpers in knots. I shoot my last signal flare away from the cliffs.

The thrall of a current and tide takes hold of *Fishing Fever*. Inexorably, the water draws the boat toward the line of surf on the rock reef just under the cliffs. That is where I am heading. I can hear the surf collide with the rocks. I can smell the land, as if the violence of the sea against the rocks has produced its own stench. The air, filled with the sea, smells of heavy brine. I estimate forty minutes before I will be in the surf against the rocks. There can be no recovery there, no sandy beaches, no gradual bottom, indeed, no beaches, just rocks sticking out of the waves like blades, and beyond, a wall of rock against which the water explodes.

I must slow my boat's drift. It is too deep here for an anchor to grip and hold on the bottom. I tie lines around two buckets, which I throw out as impromptu sea anchors. Their drag is imperceptible in these swells, which are getting higher with every ten feet I drift toward the rock wall. As I watch the buckets drag behind *Fishing Fever*, I look back in the direction where I came from. It is at that instant that I see a flare. But I do not see a boat under the flare. I am as certain as ever that I saw a flare. And if that is true, then that boat must have seen mine. The worst case, of course, would be if the boat in the distance that fired the flare was in trouble and in no position to come to my aid. That does not seem likely. But a flare is never to be fired only as an indicator; it should be ignited only if the boat firing the flare is in an emergency.

I watch helplessly. Everything is drenched. Nothing within my control can prevent from happening what I fear second only to the boat sinking under me. I will ride the boat into the reef, and if *Fishing Fever* does not beak up there, throwing me into the water, the swells will hammer her against the cliff walls. What that means for me is obvious. I will be cast into the water. I refuse to believe I will drown. The rocks can beat me to a pulp but I will survive. I am drifting to a place with no refuge.

I can see no harm in setting my Danforth. The water here may still be too deep, but the anchor will set, when the bottom shallows nearer the shore. I crawl along the starboard rail, and when I reach the bow deck I get down on my hands and knees for stability. The boat rocks and heaves and bucks. I tie the line to the cleat and over goes the anchor as I pay out scope. While I am still on the bow I look toward the sea. There is nothing out there. I scuttle back along the rail to the deck and the wheelhouse.

I scan the shore for a beach. I feel better when I strap on the revolver and holster, which allow me the illusion of independent action. Only pockets of beach punctuate this stretch of the Cape. A beach would offer me only different challenges. The boat would scrape through the reef and drift up on a narrow gravel strand. But brown bears crowd these beaches this time of year, and in minutes they would sniff out the salmon in my tanks. I cannot imagine holding off three or four of the largest bears on the planet with a revolver.

I feel the boat shudder and jump as the anchor scrapes bottom and grabs. The seabed along this coast consists mainly of clay and sand and some rock, but the Danforth is no match for the size of the swells that yank the boat against the anchor line with a loud snap. No shallow, gradual bottom gentles the sea to cliff walls. I look up at the rock face tangled with ice. I am no more than forty yards off the rocks.

Here's what it comes down to: heaven and hell. They are this close. You can be in heaven or hell and what separates them is the space between my thumb and forefinger pressed together. It's that close out here. That is what brings me out. I light my last Winston as if it were the final smoke of the condemned. I look down at the bumpers to figure out how I can work the rope under my arms and hope for the best once I am in the water. I can survive the cold if I can get in without being battered. Maybe the bumpers will overcome the force of the sea. The bumpers are my last best hope.

I would like to think this is not happening to *me*. This happens only to other fishermen. I can see my future in front of me. There is no alternative action I can take that I have not already tried. The seas will not shift, nor the wind, or current or tides to save me. No miracle is going to come my way. A finger of land juts into the water, and the sea beats at it. I am between a rock and a watery place. I came out only to catch red salmon. That was all I had on my mind. I did not care if I caught sockeye, either. I do not fish salmon to catch salmon. I mean, salmon is not the point; it provides me with an occasion. The fishing camp—the first rule is that there *is* no fishing camp—draws me out each summer, the guys, the drinking, women now and then, the bullshit and laughter, with some sockeye fishing as a diversion and excuse. I bet that the guys' stomachs are hurting with laughter about now. I thought if it ever came to this, the Bering Sea in winter would be my executioner, not the rocks off Cape Douglas. I look up in the sky to the south, in the direction of Kodiak, praying for a H-60 helicopter with the orange stripe marking of the Coast Guard to lift me out of this mess. The sky is empty.

The Danforth slips. I can feel the boat move under me with

renewed lightness. The anchor grabs and I lose my balance and hold on. The flukes are skipping along the bottom but the power of the swells pulls the anchor loose before it can dig in and hold. The scope should help the anchor purchase in the mud but no anchor was ever designed to withstand a heaving sea like this one. It slips. . . . it holds. With the swells the anchor will kite into shore. It slips again, and *Fishing Fever* continues its shoreward drift. I know I can't swim out of this. I see and hear and smell the shore and unreasonably those senses give me false hope. Land means safety from sea. But who am I fooling? Waves are too big for me to land on a beach, even if there were a beach. I would have to ride the boat in. But facing a rock wall, I am done. There is nowhere to swim. I can try to jump on a rock or cling to the cliff, but that is dreaming.

I deny the Cape my attention and turn my back on the land. I will not watch the collision. I reach down, and in a wetbag I throw a blanket, some fishing line, and my knife, and I unbuckle and place in the bag the gun belt and gun. I stuff in my Bic, a firesteel, and a towel. I close the bag tight and as I turn in the wheelhouse, I see a boat coming straight toward me. A flare lifts off—another one, and another. I leave the wheelhouse and dance a jig on the deck. Whoever is in that boat sees me, knows me, and is speeding to rescue me. I look between the land and the sea, between the cliffs and this other boat. It looks like Dino's *Rivers End*. He must have been searching since yesterday morning. I *knew* it would happen. He will not get here a minute too soon. . . .

But he could get here a minute too late. The closer to the shore, the heavier swells saw in and out swinging the boat, but more in with each cycle than out. I can feel the tug. The land is winning over the sea as if it were hungry for *Fishing Fever*. Like I said, death in one form or another, without being too melodramatic, is what this life is about. It is. It just is. I never thought that the land would be trying to kill me and the sea would be trying to kill me at the same time. This struggle is as raw as it comes.

Murphy is working his law overtime. With a slam and a shudder of the hull, the impact of the rudder against a sunken rock shoves the rudder into the stern tube and the boat begins to leak in her rear lazarette. She is quickly bogging in the stern. I open the lazarette to look at the damage knowing I have no electricity to drive the bilge pumps. I get on my knees with a coffee can bending into the compartment. There is more water coming in than I can get out. Bailing is a waste of time, because the boat will not sink from a leak in the rudder tube; it will go down from the damage to the hull against the rocks.

The *Rivers End* is turning. Dino is going to let the swells push him into me and control his speed and direction with his throttles. If he hits the rocks we are both gone. I certainly cannot save *him*. I can take a tow from either bow or stern. It looks like my bow is turning partway out of the trough, pointing closer to Dino's stern than away from it. Right now I do not worry about rigging the tow with his stern in line with my bow. I do not care where I cleat down his line as long as he can drag me back out into deeper water. He is preparing a heaving line with a monkey's head. I hastily get my knife out of the wet bag to cut the anchor line when and if I can cleat down his towing line.

He throws the line just as a swell bucks me upward in the bow. My hands are freezing and I am being thrown around. I miss the monkey's head, which plops into the water. I bend way over the bow rail to reach for it but it is too far.

He has one last shot, and he is pulling the line like a sonofabitch to get it back in quickly. I crawl back to the stern and pry off my pike pole from the clips on the deck, then inch along the starboard rail to the bow again with the pole in one hand. He is readying to throw the heaving line. I look back over my shoulder. This throw will be the last. Or we will both be in trouble. I get on my knees. I can feel *Fishing Fever* touching on the stern. *Rivers End* has turned into the trough. He is doing what has to be done. Another wave hits us.

He throws the line, which lands in the water off my bow. I jab at the monkey fist with the pike pole and bring the light line toward me. I reach over and touch the line and hold tight. I reel it in and cleat off the heavier line. With my knife I cut the anchor line, which falls away.

I yell, "Go! Go!"

He needs a few seconds to take up slack with his throttles. He does not want to foul the towing line in his wheel, not this close to deliverance. He uses the deck station to maneuver his boat, working the throttles until *Rivers End* is heading into the swells and the line is taut. Then he guns the engine. The line strains. He tows me about a hundred yards off and into deeper waters. We are still in a world of shit. It is a fourteen-mile jog over to the Barren Islands and I have water in my rear lazarette. I do not want to abandon *Fishing Fever.* I crawl back from the bow to the deck. I know that Dino has long jumper cables on his boat that I can use to juice my batteries at least enough to use the pumps, and we can skip the Barrens for Kasilof, where they will pull *Fishing Fever* out of the water and fix the fried gear.

I yell over to him to throw the cables. He is standing in his stern. I look closely at my rescuer for the first time. I should not be as surprised as I feel. I yell out to him, "Hey, what took you so long, Russ?"

We both laugh a psychotic, not a funny, laugh, until our sides ache.

Epilogue

Andy

First, the important event in 2008:

Johnathan and I, along with *Time Bandit*'s crew, shot seven miles (150 cans) of Silly String in twenty minutes in the bar of the Grand Aleutian Hotel in Dutch on Halloween last year. We assaulted the crew of the *Cornelia Marie*, who weighed in with a few cans but couldn't match us for pure fire power, and they quickly begged for mercy. We celebrated on October 13, because switched around 13 is 31 and we were out fishing on the 31st. Johnathan dressed up as a cop and I went as a convict. Eddie was Venom (Black Spider-Man). We were playing to our fantasies, or our worst nightmares. I don't know which. Johnathan's friend, who flew in for the party from Anchorage, won a free night in the Grand Aleutian for Best Costume. She came as a saucy, a *very* saucy cop. I don't know why so many people dressed up as police. As a convict, I covered my arms—no, pretty much my whole body—in jailhouse (temporary) tats. I was an artist's canvas of skulls and knives and dragons.

The night kicked off our 2008–2009 crabbing season, and from the first day out, the sea was good to us and the prayers of people for calm seas and full pots were heard. We got the full pots, and if we didn't get calm seas, we avoided the worst of the weather in ways that seemed eerie, looking back. In 120-knot blows we'd by chance be in harbor unloading, while the rest of the fleet was out getting slammed.

For king crabs, we had a quota of 240,000 pounds. We caught 240,000 pound in four days! In previous years, if we caught 90,000 pounds of king crabs in three days that would have been huge. In, 2008, we brought up 420,000 pounds in the same time, almost. The killer out there last fall was the cost of diesel. We were paying $4.50 a gallon for diesel. A full 20,000-gallon tank on *Time Bandit* costs $90,000, when only four years ago it was $20,000. The faster we could fill our tanks with crabs, the less fuel we used. We took the boat from Homer to Dutch Harbor and worked the king crab season on a single tank of diesel.

The reason for this savings, other than luck in finding crab "hot spots" quickly, was that we essentially had a new *Time Bandit* to work on this year. After the season ended, we took the boat down to a shipyard in Seattle where in dry dock we installed new fuel vents and fuel pipes made out of stainless steel, and we cleaned out the tanks. We painted the boat, inside and out, and painted the Jolly Roger (skull and bones) on the bow. We redid the rudders and our electronics, which were wired wrong in the original construction with 220 kicking over to 440, so that everything we plugged in, more or less, smoked. Finally, we put a 6-foot round by 8-foot long steel bulb on the bow that gave us 20,000 pounds of lift against the sea.

The boat had reached a point of no return after seventeen years without a refit. In a 120-knot blowup near the Pribilofs, Johnathan and I were scared. Just before we took her to the shipyard a couple of storms caught us. Our alarms were going off. We took on water, and water seeped in one of our fuel tanks. We should not have let the boat deteriorate to that point. And as Johnathan said with ironclad logic, "When I'm getting scared on the *Time Bandit*, it's time to go to the shipyard."

We did not want to spend $350,000, but we did not want to die out there either, and the price was cheap for our comfort and safety. Not only that, the refit improved the boat's speed 1 knot faster with the engine turning 150 RPMs slower.

A big bonus for us as captains was the return of our friend and old crewman Mike Fourtner, who had been with us for years and years. He was one of our better guys, and he ran the boat in salmon season in Bristol Bay. He is happy and optimistic, and he's gung-ho. If something needs doing, bam! He's on it. He does not have a drinking problem. He does not whine. And he can take charge. He'd married and decided to give up crab fishing; it was hard for us to believe. Once you are a crab fisherman city life usually is not an option. He was working in Washington as a meter reader for a year and a half. It took him that long to get a reality check. He was earning $40,000 a year, and when he decided to return to the sea, his father-in-law said he was making a real mistake. He would lose, for instance, a pension he'd receive in thirty years and, of course, health benefits; Mike said, "Screw that." And he came back.

When Neal was married in Homer on April 15, which was also the opening day of the *Deadliest Catch* 2008 season, we called his celebration "The Deadliest Wedding." Fourtner had just come back for king crab in October 2008. We planned to hit him in the face with a whipped cream pie as he was coming out of the shower. What we didn't know was that, while we were preparing the whip cream pie, Mikey went to his room, and Neal's new bride slipped into the bathroom. As she was coming out, thinking she was Mike, I slammed her with a cream pie in the face. Embarrassed, I was standing there like a little kid and she was like a deer in the headlights. Nobody's safe on the *Time Bandit*. Mikey also got 300 gallons of water poured on him. A welcome back Hillstrand style.

About that time, the start of the Opilio season, we made a bet for $1,000 with three other boats about which crew could pull the most crab pounds in any five pots in a row, with the winnings going to the crew. *Time Bandit* won. And we pulled in to port at the Pribilof Islands to celebrate. After an evening of hard drinking as we sat in Eddie's cabin on the boat, I reminded him of a wrestling match between us ten years before, when Eddie was working on our boat. At that time, he forced my knee up to my nose, and my hip hasn't been the same since. I started seeing stars go by. I reached up under his arm and gave him a bloody nose and, for a minute, we got into it. It ended in a standoff. No big deal. So, in the Pribilofs in his room, I said to him, "Remember how ten years ago you put my knee up to my nose?" The next thing, he had my knee up to my nose again. He put me in a cradle lock and threw me across the room and my head hit the light and was cut open. The wrestling turned serious for a few seconds. I was feeling no pain. I grabbed him in a guillotine, and I choked him, and in five seconds he was unconscious. I didn't know that. I let him go and he fell over like a tree and hit something and cut his head open. You could say that it was all in good fun, except for those few seconds.

After that first load of king crabs, we emptied the tanks at the Peter Pan Seafood processors in King Cove. We were tied up to the dock and lo and behold, I looked out the wheelhouse window and there was my old buddy Wild Bill, who I had not seen in six years. He was running a boat called the *Kodiak*. Wild Bill lives down in San Carlos, in Sonora, Mexico. He had extended us a standing invitation. That day he said, " I'm going home in three months. There's a marlin tournament, so why don't you guys come down and get in it with me?"

Usually we would just blow him off. But Johnathan said, "We always wanted to go marlin fishing with Bill. If we don't do it now, we're never going to."

Maybe we are more acutely aware than ever before that, given what we do, we never know if we are going to be around one year to the next. Johnathan had his warnings. He had a gall bladder attack that'd put him on the bathroom floor with pain and nearly killed him. Surgeons removed his gall bladder and found twenty stones, and they said that he could have died. And last year even more tragedy than usual visited the Bering Sea, with the sinking of the big factory boat, *Alaska Ranger*. Four men drowned in the icy waters and the Coast Guard pulled out fifty-two others who were spread out over a mile of rough sea. Twenty or thirty more of them probably would have drowned if the captain had not told them to abandon ship when he did. As soon as he threw the engines in reverse, the boat sank. And if the sea wasn't lethal enough for one year, we had several guys drown last year right in Dutch Harbor falling in the water between boats, like Johnathan did on Halloween when he went back to *Time Bandit* for his Silly String. The men who died, no one heard their screams. The same would have happened to John, if the *Time Bandit*'s crew had not been watching him from the car on the dock. He could have hit his head on the way down. People say that they are praying for us, and it works. We had no injuries except Eddie's broken foot, and bumps and bruises. Johnathan went out on deck and threw the hook underneath the horn of the block. The 12-pound hook swung back and hit him in the nose, which bled really good but wasn't broken.

We decided to seize the opportunity to fish for marlin, and

just so that nobody could get shanghaied by wives and girl-friends, we flew straight from King Cove, and twenty-four hours later we were in Tucson with Wild Bill driving over the Mexican border in his white truck. The next day we were fishing in the Sea of Cortez aboard a 65-foot Viking owned by Morgan, a friend of Wild Bill. We went out in 14-foot seas, and Morgan said, "I'd never come out in weather like this, usually." It was normal weather for us. We put our feet up and drank beer in the stern, like it was sunny and dead calm.

At some point, around a hundred dolphins started chasing tuna in front of us. We stopped for them. We circled around and the next thing we knew the tuna were racing toward us. We had three or four hookups at the same time and suddenly were throwing the tuna, several at once, over the gunwales, while in water that was up to our thighs. The Mexican deck hand was shitting his pants because of the rough sea. We caught fifteen tuna before we stopped, and we could have caught more.

We fished that day and came back in and planned on going out the next morning. The sea was still rough but it was forecast to calm down. We stayed out for an hour and said screw this. Wild Bill and his wife keep horses. And while Johnathan and our brother Neal and a couple other guys went to a cantina, I rode down the beach over the dunes and in the water, ending in town where I tied my horse to a rail and walked in the cantina bare-foot.

It was beautiful.

During the year, when we were not fishing, our travels to pro-mote the *Deadliest Catch* took Johnathan and me through Europe. Johnathan and Russell went to Sweden. They visited bars. In one, Russell met an American whose ex-girlfriend was Russell's old girlfriend's sister in Coeur d'Aelene, Idaho. Russell started a street brawl with a crowd of Turks who were marching down a street with trumpets and flags celebrating a soccer victory. He grabbed one of their flags, and the Turks came after him and he wouldn't give it up.

Before Stockholm, Johnathan and Russell went to Copenhagen. The police kicked them out of the city for being too loud. Laughing too much with Russell I guess is against the law there.

Later, Johnathan and I visited London together for three days for their *Deadliest Catch* season premiere. We visited all the sights. The people were geat. That's about all we can say about London. We had a brilliant time.

And when I finally came home to Southern Indiana, my wife Sabrina and I decided to list our modest horse farm, Hobby Horse Acres, for sale. I want to downsize my life, which was becoming too complicated, with promoting the show and stuff. Our horse business took off better than I dreamed, and I did not have the time to devote to it, without becoming a slave to it. It has seventeen acres, a covered horse arena, thirteen horse stalls, our house, and a small lake. If you want to buy the place, give me a call.

That is about all we have to tell you. We are about to leave for Dutch Harbor to begin the 2009 Opilio season. I hope the seas are kind to us, but that is only something we can pray for, but not expect. The sea is what brings us out fishing season after season. Johnathan and I are not getting younger, and I would like to think we are getting wiser, but as you have just read, I'd only be kidding myself if I said we were. We are fishermen. We are as stuck with the sea as it is with us. Johnathan's son Scotty, who joined us last year as a permanent member of our crabbing crew said to me, about his father, "I love my Dad more than I hate him." That pretty much sums up how Johnathan and I feel about the sea.

Acknowledgments

We could easily crowd the deck of *Time Bandit* with the people to whom we owe a debt of gratitude for getting us to and through this book. In this long procession, we have to start with our mother, Joan, who sewed us up all the times we got cut, and gave us her mother's love; and our stepdad, Bob Phillips, who put up with our misbehavior and taught us and protected us. Our brother Neal deserves our thanks for being such a great brother; we could not do any of what we do without him. Joe and Arlene McDougall in Seattle and Deedee in Homer keep the wolves from our doors with their bookkeeping for *Time Bandit*.

We have had some great crews on *Time Bandit* over the years, but none quite to equal Russell Newberry, a friend from way back. We want to thank the many fishermen who have worked with us. We offer our respects to those who are no longer with us, Clark Sparks and Mike Lyda, who drowned doing what they loved. Our hearts go out to the families of the men whom the sea has taken away, especially the captain of the *Troika* and the other doomed sailors mentioned in this book.

Thank you, Dino Sutherland, for providing your boat, *Rivers Edge*, to come to Johnathan's rescue.

We are indebted to the good folks at the Discovery Channel,

including Amy Hagovsky, who handles the channel's publicity/ press, and George Neighbors, Discovery's director of talent/ management. Thanks as well to Thom Beers, Jeff Conroy, and Matt Renner at Original Productions, and all their camera crews who have been on *Time Bandit*. You know who you are.

We owe a tremendous debt to all the people whose stories we tell in this book.

At Random House, we thank Will Murphy for seeing this project clearly from the start, and his assistant, Lea Beresford, who put all the parts together. Without our agents, Alan Nevins and Mindy Stone at the Firm, this book would never have come about; they have been tireless, and we cannot thank them enough. Their humor, dedication, and resolve have carried us over several obstacles. They are the best the profession has to offer. Finally, thanks to Malcolm, who traveled the Bering Sea with us in good humor and who, with a hook of curiosity, reeled in this book from an ocean of stories and tales.

And let's not forget to thank Mother Nature, the best teacher we've ever had, and God, for keeping us alive against some stacked odds.

The new chapter in *Time Bandit* was also Malcolm's last. Our good friend passed away a few days after putting this together for us. We will miss you, our friend, for you embraced life. You showed us how to say "I love you" to those close to us and how to enjoy the little things to the fullest. It's not often that you meet people who change your life, but Malcolm, you were one of them. Safe journey to you, our friend. God bless you from Andy & Johnathan and the *Time Bandit* crew.

On board *Time Bandit*, their family-owned and -operated vessel, brothers **Johnathan** and **Andy Hillstrand** share the skippering duties. Johnathan, a resident of Homer, Alaska, takes the helm during the king crab season. When not on deck, he can usually be found on the back of his Harley Fat Boy. During opilio season, Andy sits in the wheelhouse. In the off-season, he can be found training horses on his ranch in Indiana.

Malcolm MacPherson was a correspondent for *Newsweek* and the author of more than a dozen books, including most recently the satirical war novel *Hocus Potus* and *Roberts Ridge*, a nonfiction account of battle in Afghanistan. He lived near the Blue Ridge Mountains in Virginia with his wife and children until his death in 2009.